THE WORLDS OF
SHERLOCK
HOLMES

THE WORLDS OF
SHERLOCK
HOLMES

THE INSPIRATION
BEHIND THE WORLD'S GREATEST DETECTIVE

ANDREW LYCETT

FRANCES
LINCOLN

INTRODUCTION

Welcome to *The Worlds of Sherlock Holmes*! This book intends to put the great detective's life into context – to explore the places where he lived and operated; to sketch in the political and social background to his era; to show how the business of detection developed and how he went about it; to examine the intellectual underpinnings of the late Victorian culture he experienced (principally relating to science); to show how his reputation has continued to flourish so widely since the death of his ultimate creator Sir Arthur Conan Doyle in 1930, with particular reference to the ways in which he has been portrayed on film and other media; and also to investigate a few niche areas where his interests are worthy of note, including sport, art and publishing.

Sherlock Holmes, the man, was something of an enigma. He was a brilliant and energetic consulting detective, who built a career on watching the world for trifles and using what he observed to deduce what happened in a variety of usually criminal situations. But after putting away his magnifying glass, he was personally self-effacing, liking to hide away in his Baker Street lodgings, sometimes not even bothering to emerge from his room to eat. He was not totally socially inept, but he preferred solitary pleasures such as reading and playing his violin. If bored and missing the stimulation of the detailed brainwork involved in his investigations, or simply when depressed by the relentless London fog, he would – to the consternation of his companion Dr John Watson – inject himself with a 7 per cent solution of cocaine. He was generally good-natured, but just occasionally his behaviour became alarming, as when he would sit in an armchair with his hair-trigger gun and amuse himself by marking out the letters V.R. (for Victoria Regina) with the shots he fired into the opposite wall.

Today we might describe him as bipolar, someone prone to spectacular mood swings, 'alternating', as Dr Watson observed, 'from week to week between cocaine and ambition, the drowsiness of the drug, and the fierce energy of his own keen nature.' But that inconsistency makes him interesting. (It is indeed the trait which animates the popular BBC television series *Sherlock*, starring Benedict Cumberbatch.) It helps explain how this 'calculating machine', who spurned female company and whom Watson described as being 'positively inhuman … at times', could enter the minds of the most bizarre criminals. He prided

Oppsosite The June 1891 issue of The Strand Magazine, *which featured 'A Scandal in Bohemia'.*

himself on his scientific approach to problem-solving, and that was what defined him. But he could supplement that with extraordinary intuition. When he wants to praise Inspector Baynes in 'The Adventure of Wisteria Lodge', Holmes tells him he will rise high in his profession because he has 'instinct and intuition' – attributes clearly as important to his own investigative techniques as his rationality, if not trumpeted as much.

In this respect Holmes mirrors his age. As will become clear in the succeeding chapters, he flourished in the late nineteenth century when the spirit of rationality carried all before it. Modern science, in the form of physics, chemistry, biology, and more abstruse specialities such as geology, opened up the secrets of the material universe and put them to the use of humanity. It was a time of exploration and expansiveness, not just of knowledge, but also of the globe.

But such advances brought a backlash. By the 1890s, when Holmes was at his most incisive, new forces were already emerging in society. Having studied with the French neurologist Jean-Martin Charcot in Paris in 1886, the Austrian Sigmund Freud in Vienna was beginning to develop the practice of psychoanalysis, with its underlying theories of the unconscious mind. The scientific ideas

underlying much of Holmes's methodology were under threat from fresh approaches to physics, notably the development of quantum theory by the German physicist Max Planck in 1900, the announcement of the special theory of relativity by the Austrian Albert Einstein in 1905, leading, at the very end of Holmes's published life, to the introduction of the uncertainty principle by Werner Heisenberg, another German, in 1927. While remaining true to his own precepts, Holmes, with his curious sensitivity, could not help but reflect some of this cultural background. With his avowed Bohemianism, there was even a hint of contemporary dandyish decadence in his approach to life.

In this he had certain similarities to his creator. Arthur Conan Doyle was admittedly far removed from *fin de siècle* aestheticism and nothing in his life suggested any enthusiasm for the ideas of either Freud or Einstein. But curiously, although deeply committed to the practices of a scientist through his training as a doctor in Edinburgh, Conan Doyle had his own issues with the science of his day. He could never quite give up the idea that there was another dimension to existence, something more deeply interfused – an attitude which, for all his claims to agnosticism, looked back to his Roman Catholic upbringing. In particular, he could never reconcile himself to Freud's mechanistic model of the mind; he believed it should include some element of the spirit, or soul. So, after biding his time, he came out as a spiritualist, which he promoted as a science. And, never doing anything by halves, he became perhaps the world's greatest exponent of the possibilities of the paranormal.

So, both the creator and his subject had their rationality challenged from outside. Of course, they were very different, as Conan Doyle once forcibly pointed out in a poem 'To an Undiscerning Critic':

> *So please grip this fact with your cerebral tentacle,*
> *The doll and its maker are never identical.*

The closing couplet was a rejoinder to a detractor who suggested that because Sherlock Holmes had disparaged Edgar Allan Poe's detective Auguste Dupin, he too must have been averse to this Parisian advocate of ratiocination.

The focus of this book is, however, largely on the fictional Sherlock Holmes, and the world that shaped him and how he represented it. He lived on Baker Street in more or less the centre of London, the city whose quirky, restless energy permeates his stories. London gave them a special sense of place. It was the centre of the world's most powerful economy which had grown, along with Britain's colonial boundaries and cultural influence (its hard and its soft power), on the back of scientific discoveries, many of them made over the previous few decades and very often at home.

That economy flourished partly as the result of the good luck of having access to appropriate natural resources. But it also reflected the stable political environment that allowed it to thrive. Sherlock Holmes himself was not much of a political beast. As weighed up in 'Britain and the Wider World' (pages 43–68), he was a traditionally minded liberal imperialist who nevertheless used his calling to further the cause of justice where he could, sometimes even taking it into his own hands and allowing suspects to walk free. His lifestyle was related – old fogeyish, with that touch of the Bohemianism acknowledged in his exploits. It reflected the masculine culture of the times when women played little part in public life, let alone had the vote. Holmes preferred his own company, or, if necessary, that of other men, such as the amenable Dr Watson.

Opposite Benedict Cumberbatch as the consulting detective in BBC TV's Sherlock *(2010–17).*

Left Portrait of Sir Arthur Conan Doyle from Play Pictorial, *1909.*

This has led to suggestions that Holmes might be gay, a reading sometimes supported by reference to his concern when Watson is slightly wounded in a confrontation in 'The Adventure of the Three Garridebs' and to Watson's response, 'It was worth a wound – it was worth many wounds – to know the depth of loyalty and love which lay behind that cold mask.' But this is nothing more than a Victorian bromance. Watson is happily married to Mary Morstan, the elegant woman he met early on in *The Sign of Four*. The only interest that Holmes showed in the opposite sex was in Irene Adler, whom he confronted in 'A Scandal in Bohemia', and referred to as 'always the woman'. But as Watson himself explained, 'It was not that he felt any emotion akin to love for Irene Adler. All emotions, and that one particularly, were abhorrent to his cold, precise but admirably balanced mind. He was, I take it, the most perfect reasoning and observing machine that the world has seen, but as a lover he would have placed himself in a false position. He never spoke of the softer passions, save with a gibe and a sneer.' That final observation is off-putting, but underlines the underlying truth – for Holmes, the demands of his profession took precedence over any sexual needs. As he himself admitted,

'Women have seldom been an attraction to me, for my brain has always governed my heart.'

However, Holmes is always respectful of the members of the female sex he encounters in his casework. He may have had little time personally for the softer passions, but he understands and accepts the power of strong emotion, recognizing, for example, how Captain Croker's love for Lady Brackenstall in 'The Adventure of the Abbey Grange' may have driven him to murder, and declining to pass judgment (as other Victorians might have done) when dealing with adulterous relationships, such as that of Mary Browner (*née* Cushing) in 'The Adventure of the Cardboard Box'.

Having examined how Holmes fares in politics and society, this book addresses how he absorbed the monumental scientific advances of his age. In this field, perhaps more than anywhere, he drew on the lived experiences of his begetter – Arthur Conan Doyle. And this leads to a survey of detection, the very core of Holmes's being. He lives for his work. So, the origins of his profession are assessed (for a long time, detectives weren't welcomed by the general public), along with the parallel rise of detective fiction, and how Conan Doyle himself fits into the picture.

Right 'Holmes examines the corpse', a 1904 illustration by Sidney Paget for 'The Adventure of the Abbey Grange'.

Opposite Alphonse Bertillon's 1909 'Synoptic Table of Physiognomic Traits' was a tool widely used by the police for describing and classifying faces and bodies.

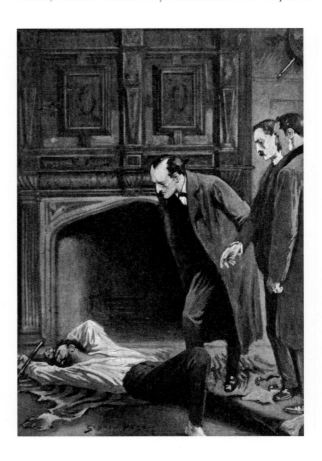

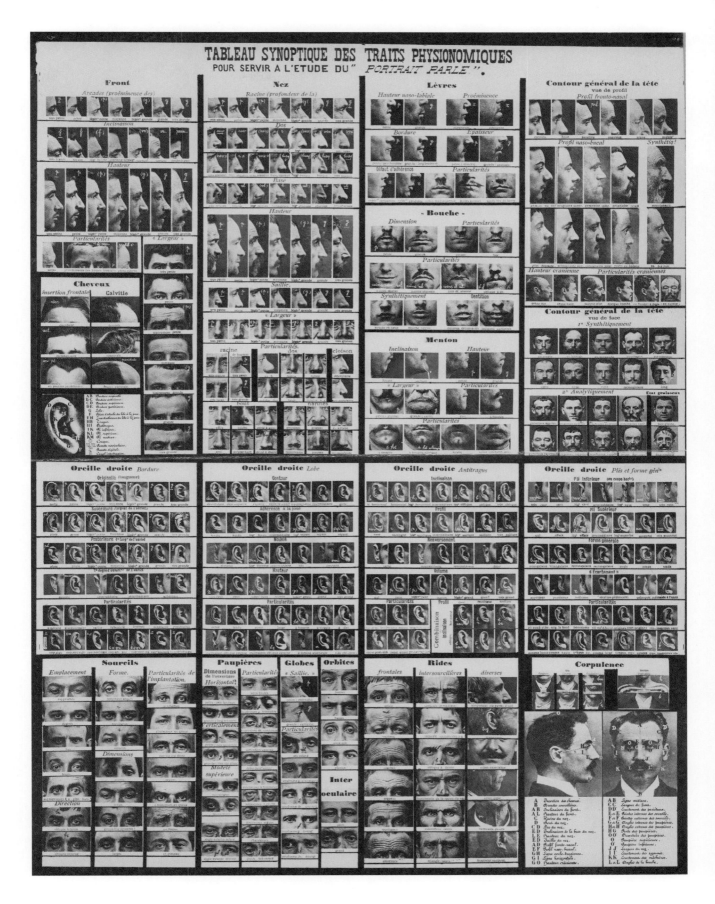

TABLEAU SYNOPTIQUE DES TRAITS PHYSIONOMIQUES
POUR SERVIR A L'ETUDE DU " PORTRAIT PARLE ".

For all his training, Holmes turns out to be fairly low-tech exponent of his trade – observing always; showing off his skills as a chemist; keeping up with the latest developments, but never rushing to implement them (particularly if they are foreign, such as the anthropometrics of Alphonse Bertillon or the crude profiling pioneered by Cesare Lombroso). The restrained cerebral approach remains paramount.

More than with most literary figures, Holmes's name has not only survived, but remained globally famous over the years. So, this book takes time to examine two particular aspects of his posthumous life – one, how he has been portrayed on the stage and in particular on film (usually very successfully), and the other relating to the way his reputation has been enhanced through a combination of scholarship, clubs (known in the Sherlockian world as 'scion societies'), fans (with their 'fanfics'), statues and assorted memorabilia.

Some shorter chapters look at features of the detective that might otherwise be glossed over. One looks at the publishing world that brought him to prominence, with particular reference to *The Strand Magazine* which – with their defining illustrations by Sidney Paget – introduced his exploits to hundreds of thousands of eager readers. Holmes's well-informed attitudes to sport and to art are also explored.

Underlying all is the sheer brilliance of Conan Doyle's (or, for some readers, Watson's) portrayal of Holmes's world. In the words of John le Carré, who knew a thing or two about writing, this works because of 'a kind of narrative perfection: a perfect interplay between dialogue and description, perfect characterization and perfect timing'. According to Le Carré, this allows the Holmes stories to be translated without loss into practically any language.

The overriding focus of this book, however, is that Sherlock Holmes was a metonym for his inquisitive age. He represents his times, with their respect for the merits of close observation, their enthusiasm for discovery, their confidence in the accumulation of knowledge, and their sense of the exciting new possibilities, both physical and intellectual.

A SHERLOCKIAN
SENSE OF PLACE

You can't have Sherlock Holmes without London. It is the city where the famous consulting detective lives, dreams and, crucially, conducts his business. His adventures show off the British capital in all its splendour and diversity, transporting readers from the grand mansions of Hampstead to the slums of the East End, taking in notable locations such as Trafalgar Square and the Strand, with the magnificent River Thames flowing down the middle. And a little at a tangent, but the hub for Holmes, was 221B Baker Street, where the lodgings which he shared for at least part of the time with Dr John Watson stand.

This great metropolis is introduced by Watson in *A Study in Scarlet* at the start of the canon as, 'that great cesspool into which all the loungers and idlers of the Empire are irresistibly drained'. Inevitably this imperial magnet attracts a colourful range of aristocrats, scoundrels, foreigners and natives, whose exploits go to make the Holmes stories so rich and entertaining.

The first place in London specifically mentioned in those fifty-six stories and four novels is the Criterion Bar, a popular meeting place on Piccadilly Circus, where

Left St Paul's and Ludgate Hill, *oil and canvas, by William Logsdail (1859–1944).*

Dr Watson, newly arrived from Afghanistan, runs into his old dresser, Stamford, and asks advice about a possible place to live. He is directed to meet Sherlock Holmes in his laboratory in St Bartholomew's Hospital, two miles to the east, on the edge of the actual City of London. A plaque at the Criterion commemorates this fictional encounter, dating it, on the evidence of the story, to New Year's Day 1881. The real-life building had been opened seventeen years earlier during the great mid-century expansion of the city as part of a large Byzantine-inspired theatre/restaurant complex, designed by the architect Thomas Verity (who was also responsible for the Pavilion at Lord's Cricket Ground, a venue much loved by Holmes's author Conan Doyle).

As agreed, Watson presents himself the next day at Holmes's lodgings in Baker Street. The Metropolitan underground line can be viewed from the sitting room, which is an advantage. Otherwise, there's not much description in the canon of the immediate environs, apart from a reference in 'A Case of Identity' to a 'dull neutral-tinted London street'. John Fisher Murray described Baker Street in his popular 1843 guidebook *The World of London* as one of the city's 'high genteel neighbourhoods … The people inhabiting this class of neighbourhood are

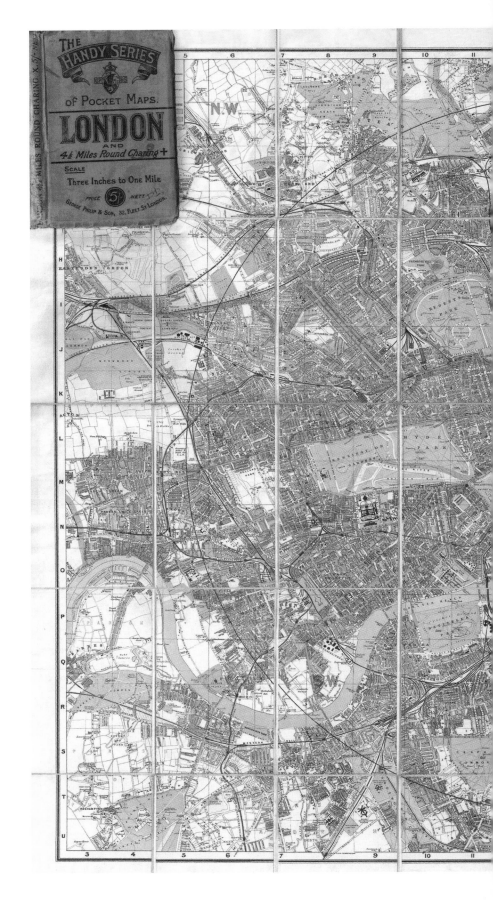

Right *Philip Pocket Map of London, 1895.*

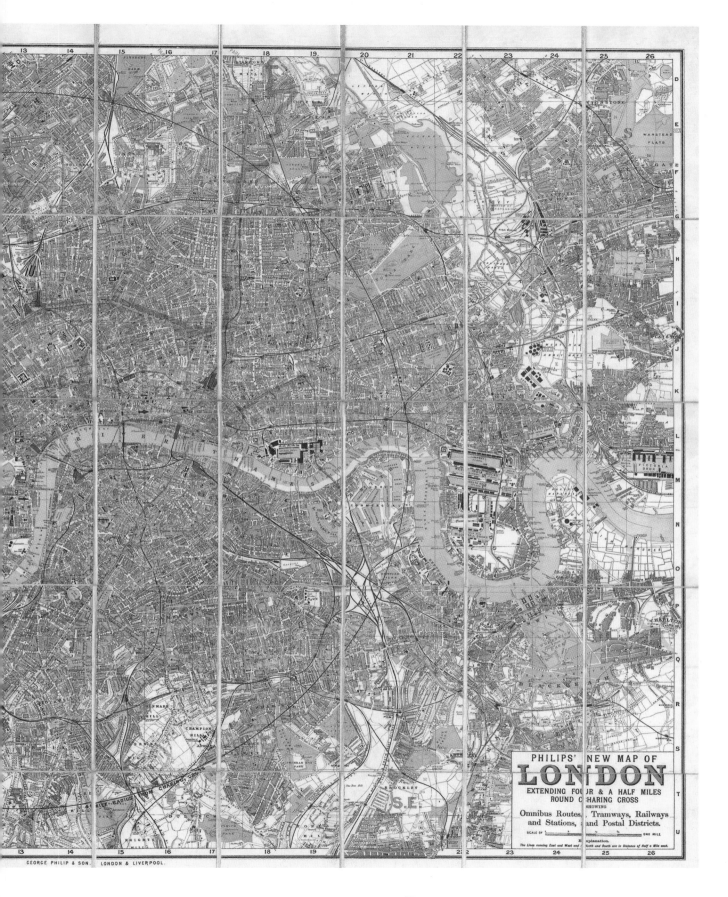

PHILIPS' NEW MAP OF
LONDON
EXTENDING FOUR & A HALF MILES
ROUND CHARING CROSS
SHOWING
Omnibus Routes, Tramways, Railways
and Stations, and Postal Districts.

SCALE OF   ONE MILE

Explanation.
The Lines running East and West and North and South are in Distance of Half a Mile each.

GEORGE PHILIP & SON. LONDON & LIVERPOOL.

usually scions of respectable, or distant connections of noble families, remarkably correct in their style of living and equipage, but evidently of slender means; however, they boast this advantage, that an educated taste can do more in this style of living with a thousand a-year, than vulgar opulence can with ten times the revenue.'

The road itself was one of several leading northwards from the West End of London, and particularly from Oxford Street, the main retail centre of the city with a growing concentration of large stores, such as Marshall & Snelgrove. Originally developed by William Baker, a builder, in the eighteenth century, the old houses around Baker Street had been demolished in the early Victorian era to allow railways access to the new station at Euston and the underground that followed later.

It was the railways which initially brought Conan Doyle himself to the area, when he travelled to London as a fifteen-year-old schoolboy during the Christmas holidays of 1874. He alighted at Euston station, one of the first mainline termini in the capital, built in 1837. He took the underground to Earl's Court, and then a cab to nearby Finborough Road, where his artist uncle Dicky lived. During his three weeks in London, Conan Doyle was taken to all the sights, including Westminster Abbey, the Tower of London, London Zoo and Crystal Palace. He also went to the theatre and to Madame Tussaud's waxworks, where he was attracted by the grim relics of the French Revolution displayed in the Chamber of Horrors (a term coined by the contemporary magazine *Punch*). At that time, the waxworks were housed above a set of buildings known as the Baker Street Bazaar.

Later, when working as a GP in Portsmouth, Conan Doyle befriended an architect, Percy Boulnois, whose father had made a fortune by developing the Baker Street Bazaar – originally the barracks for a cavalry regiment (the second troop of Horse Guards) and later a market-cum-stable for horses – into a fashionable retail arcade. Since Conan Doyle was liaising with Percy Boulnois at the same time as he was writing his first Sherlock Holmes story, *A Study in Scarlet*, it seems likely (though not anywhere confirmed) that he picked up on the Baker Street name through this connection. (Percy's brother Edmund, who ran the Baker Street Bazaar, was a prominent local JP and MP.)

During the nineteenth century, modern town houses sprouted up around Baker Street as the capital grew in size, and this particular thoroughfare allowed access

Right Piccadilly Circus and The Criterion, where Holmes and Watson first met, c.1922.

Opposite Madame Tussaud's exhibition of wax figures at the Baker Street Bazaar, 1841.

to fashionable spots, running northwards past Lord's Cricket Ground and St John's Wood. (St John's Wood, another residential area, was reputedly used by rich men to accommodate their mistresses. It was also the home of Irene Adler, whom Sherlock Holmes described ambiguously as 'the woman' and who, according to 'A Scandal in Bohemia', had a fictional address there at Briony Lodge on Serpentine Avenue.)

The outside of Holmes's house is mentioned only obliquely in 'The Adventure of the Empty House' when the detective takes an unfamiliar back-path to Baker Street to avoid unwanted followers. Watson recalls, 'Our route was certainly a singular one. Holmes's knowledge of the byways of London was extraordinary, and on this occasion he passed rapidly and with an assured step through a network of mews and stables, the very existence of which I had never known. We emerged at last into a small road, lined with old, gloomy houses, which led us into Manchester Street, and so to Blandford Street. Here he turned swiftly down a narrow passage, passed through a wooden gate into a deserted yard, and then opened with a key the back door of a house. We entered together, and he closed it behind us.' Watson is surprised to find himself looking at their own

house in Baker Street, but, as Holmes explains, the view is from Camden House on the other side of the road. (Keen Sherlockians have suggested that this association with Blandford Street puts the actual location of Holmes's house lower down Baker Street, numbered around 30.)

If the exterior of Holmes's lodgings is hazy, the interior is memorably sketched. The dwelling consists of 'a couple of comfortable bedrooms and a single large airy sitting-room, cheerfully furnished, and illuminated by two broad windows.' Orderly chaos is the design motif. But even Watson, who claims not to be particularly fussy after a career in medicine and the army, is surprised by his new friend's living habits. Holmes keeps his cigars in the coal scuttle, his tobacco in the toe of a Persian slipper and his unanswered correspondence held by a knife in the centre of his wooden mantelpiece. Papers dealing with past investigations are spread all over the place, along with evidence of the chemicals Holmes uses in his scientific research. Most bizarre of all, one of the walls is peppered with bullet holes arranged to depict a 'patriotic' V.R., in honour of the reigning queen.

Holmes certainly has an encyclopedic knowledge of the surrounding streets (usually negotiated on foot or else in a

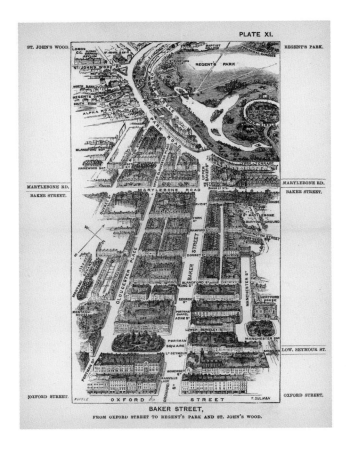

Above An illustration of Baker Street by Herbert Fry (1830–85), from London in 1888.

Opposite Baker Street, *by John Sutton (1935–).*

hansom cab). He himself boasted to Watson in 'The Red-Headed League', 'It is a hobby of mine to have an exact knowledge of London.' And, situated as he then was in that story on the edge of the City in the fictional Saxe-Coburg Square, he looked around to note some lesser-known features of the locale. 'There is Mortimer's, the tobacconist, the little newspaper shop, the Coburg branch of the City and Suburban Bank, the Vegetarian Restaurant, and McFarlane's carriage-building depot.'

In *The Sign of Four* Holmes shows off his familiarity with the wider capital on a trip to the South London home of Thaddeus Sholto. Watson reported him muttering the names of the streets:

> as the cab rattled through squares and in and out by tortuous by-streets. 'Rochester Row,' said he. 'Now Vincent Square. Now we come out on the Vauxhall Bridge Road. We are making for the Surrey side apparently. Yes, I thought so. Now we are on the bridge. You can catch glimpses of the river.' We did indeed get a fleeting view of a stretch of the Thames, with the lamps shining upon the broad, silent water; but our cab dashed on and was soon involved in a labyrinth of streets upon the other side.
>
> 'Wordsworth Road,' said my companion. 'Priory Road. Lark Hall Lane. Stockwell Place. Robert Street. Cold Harbour Lane. Our quest does not appear to take us to very fashionable regions.' We had indeed reached a questionable and forbidding neighbourhood. Long lines of dull brick houses were only relieved by the coarse glare and tawdry brilliancy of public houses at the corner. Then came rows of two-storied villas, each with a fronting of miniature garden, and then again interminable lines of new, staring brick buildings – the monster tentacles which the giant city was throwing out into the country.

Watson was referring to London's relentless expansion, which had started with the industrialization of Britain in the early nineteenth century, when people with uncertain futures on the land flocked from rural areas to the cities to find work in factories. In England and Wales, the percentage of city dwellers grew from 17 per cent in 1801 to 72 per cent in 1891. London was inevitably one of the main centres to which the rootless were attracted, even if in the last couple of decades of the 1800s this phenomenal urban growth slowed down. According to the historian Jerry White, the population of Greater London 'only' grew by 16.8 per cent in the 1890s, the slowest rate of growth since the 1830s. Even so, this figure was 4,767,000 in 1881, 5,634,000 in 1891 and 6,581,000 in 1901, an explosion which contributed to the extreme poverty of 30.7 per cent of the inhabitants surveyed in Charles Booth's sociological survey *Life and Labour of the People of London* (1886–1903).

By Holmes's day, London took in sprawling suburbs – not just those within walking or a cab journey's distance of Baker Street, such as St John's Wood or Hampstead (the seat at Appledore Towers of 'the worst man in London', the notorious blackmailer Charles Augustus Milverton in the adventure of the same name) – but those further afield, requiring transportation by train or the new underground railways, such as: Upper Norwood, where Holmes and Watson visited Bartholomew Sholto after meeting his brother Thaddeus (and close to where Conan Doyle himself lived in the 1890s); Harrow, home of Honoria Westphail, aunt of Helen Stoner, in 'The Adventure of the Speckled Band'; and all the other places such as Norbury, Esher and Croydon where canonical characters happen to live.

But since Holmes lived in central London, he was usually drawn in by investigations closer to his home, which meant those in the heart of the capital. Inevitably the original City (with a big 'C'), the so-called Square Mile where the banks and other financial institutions were concentrated, was a hotbed of what might now be called white-collar crime. Here, close to the Bank of England, stood well-known firms such as Holder & Stevenson, the City's second largest private banking business, whose senior partner Alexander Holder visits Baker Street (by Tube) to request Holmes's help after the disappearance of the Beryl Coronet in the story with that name. Within the City could also be found several established businesses, such as Westhouse & Marbank, 'the great claret importers of Fenchurch Street', referred to in 'A Case of Identity'.

Moving westwards, the centres of government and administration around Whitehall and the Houses of Parliament also attracted Holmes and his investigative services. In this area was situated Scotland Yard, the headquarters of the Metropolitan Police, where he liaised somewhat reluctantly with detectives such as Inspector Lestrade. The Foreign Office, just off Whitehall, featured in 'The Adventure of the Naval Treaty', where details

about the geography of the place, and how a clerk might evade observation, were crucial to the development of the story.

Whitehall led to Trafalgar Square, often regarded as the hub of the capital, from where neighbourhoods frequented by Holmes radiated in all directions. Directly to the east was the Strand (which gave its name to *The Strand Magazine*, which first published the Sherlock Holmes stories in 1891). Originally this street was a busy bridleway beside the Thames, linking Westminster and the City. In the Sherlock Holmes stories, Conan Doyle gave this thoroughfare a genteel makeover; Holmes and Watson liked to repair there at the end of a busy day to eat at Simpson's, a popular traditional English restaurant which was known earlier in the century as Simpson's Grand Divan Tavern. In real life, the Strand was one of the rowdiest streets in London, throbbing with public houses, theatres, music halls, cheap lodging houses and prostitution. This was partly because it was so close to Charing Cross station, one of the most used railway terminuses by the end of the century. At the attached Charing Cross Hotel, Holmes met and arrested the spy at the heart of 'The Adventure of the Bruce-Partington Plans'.

Around the corner, in Northumberland Avenue, could be found several of the more up-market hotels of the sort frequented by the wealthy foreign visitors who provided custom to Mr Melas, the translator in 'The Adventure of the Greek Interpreter'. Sir Henry Baskerville stayed at one of these, the Northumberland Hotel, when he first came to London. The theft of his tan boots there provided a vital clue to the skulduggery taking place at his ancestral home in Devon. This hostelry, which stands on the corner of the narrower Northumberland Street, adjacent to the Avenue, is sometimes identified as the Northumberland Arms, now a public house, which changed its name to the Sherlock Holmes in 1957. Close by was the Turkish Bath where Holmes and Watson liked to go, as recorded in 'The Adventure of the Illustrious Client'.

The other side of Trafalgar Square gave on to Pall Mall, home of several traditional gentlemen's clubs, including the Diogenes Club, which Holmes's brother Mycroft visited daily from his lodgings along the street. One of its rules was that members were not allowed to speak to one another, which suited the cerebral Mycroft. Conan Doyle himself was more sociable and enjoyed club life, having first made his mark on the London literary establishment as a guest

Left Trafalgar Square, *colour lithograph by Herbert Menzies Marshall (1841–1913), from* The Scenery of London *(1905).*

at the Savile Club in Brook Street in the 1880s, and later himself becoming a member of the Reform, Athenaeum and Royal Automobile Clubs – not to mention the Marylebone Cricket Club.

North from Pall Mall, the stately Regent Street runs north, past Piccadilly Circus (site of the already mentioned Criterion Bar) and then, in a gracious curve, rolling by the nearby Café Royal and the Langham Hotel, which stands close to the headquarters of the present-day British Broadcasting Corporation on Langham Place. Outside the Café Royal, Holmes was assaulted in 'The Illustrious Client' by two armed men with sticks – ruffians employed by the villainous Baron Gruner – who then disappeared in the adjoining Glasshouse Street. The café was closed in 2008, but the Langham Hotel enjoyed a revival when, after a period of inactivity as an annexe to the BBC, it reopened as a five-star luxury hotel in 1991. Just over a century earlier, on 30 August 1889, its earlier incarnation served as the venue for a momentous event in Conan Doyle's life, when he travelled from Portsmouth to dine there with Joseph M. Stoddart, editor of the Philadelphia-based *Lippincott's Monthly Magazine*, who commissioned him to write what became his second Sherlock Holmes novel, *The Sign of Four*. The success of this venture encouraged Conan Doyle to give up his practice on the south coast and move to London, albeit he initially hoped also to continue his medical career, though this time as an eye specialist. (As well as an Irish MP, the fourth guest at the dinner was the author and wit Oscar Wilde, who was also asked to write something for serialization in the *Magazine* – an undertaking which was published in book form as *The Picture of Dorian Gray*.) The hotel clearly held a fond memory for Conan Doyle, as the King of Bohemia stayed there in 'A Scandal in Bohemia', as did the Honourable Philip Green when visiting London in 'The Disappearance of Lady Frances Carfax'.

On another axis from Trafalgar Square was Covent Garden, home of the Royal Opera House, where Holmes liked to relax, even if, as in 'The Adventure of the Red Circle', pressure of work meant he could only reach his seat for the second act of a Wagner performance. Covent Garden was also a market area, noted for the sale of fruit and vegetables, as well as other foodstuffs, such as the goose which Holmes's commissionaire Peterson acquired when he witnessed an altercation in Tottenham Court Road. The detective subsequently discovered that it was part of a batch of two dozen birds purchased in Covent Garden by a member of the Christmas goose club run by drinkers

Above Oscar Wilde (1854–1900) in 1882.

at the nearby Alpha Inn. Earnest sleuths have credibly suggested that the Alpha Inn was a pub originally called the Dog and Duck and now the Museum Tavern, opposite the British Museum.

Holmes liked to use the British Museum (which then also housed its renowned Reading Room) to research topics of interest, such as voodooism, which enabled him to solve the mystery of the death of a Spaniard at Wisteria Lodge in Surrey between Esher and Oxshott. The British Museum is in the heart of Bloomsbury, home of the University of London, where both Holmes and Watson had studied (Watson more formally). When he first came to London, Holmes had also lived in Bloomsbury, in Montague Street. This is not far from Montague Place, where Conan Doyle had lodged when arriving to London from Portsmouth to pursue his career as an eye specialist; he took consulting rooms in nearby Upper Wimpole Street, which was but a short distance from Baker Street.

Running through the capital was the River Thames, a central topographical feature in the Holmes stories. It provides the backdrop in *The Sign of Four* for the exciting river chase, which would become a staple of popular thrillers, both in print and on film. In their fast police-boat,

Holmes and Scotland Yard's Athelney Jones take up the trail of the fleeing Jonathan Small at Jacobson's Yard, near Tower Bridge. Small and Tonga, his tiny Andaman Islander companion who can blow poison darts, are in the *Aurora*, said to be the quickest steam launch on the river. The places on the banks of the river hurtle past. 'We had shot through the pool, past the West India Docks, down the long Deptford Reach, and up again after rounding the Isle of Dogs … At Greenwich we were about three hundred paces behind them. At Blackwall we could not have been more than two hundred and fifty.' Finally they caught up on a clear stretch of the river, 'with Barking Level upon one side and the melancholy Plumstead Marshes upon the other.'

The river and the adjacent docks are central to London's prosperity, carrying the commodities and manufactured goods that made Britain the economic engine of the world. They are also the port of entry for large numbers of immigrants and visitors, often sailors and vagrants of the type who end up in the opium dens of the East End. The most famous of these in the Holmes canon is The Bar of Gold in Upper Swandam Lane, situated, according to Dr Watson in 'The Man with the Twisted Lip', in 'a vile alley lurking behind the high wharves which line

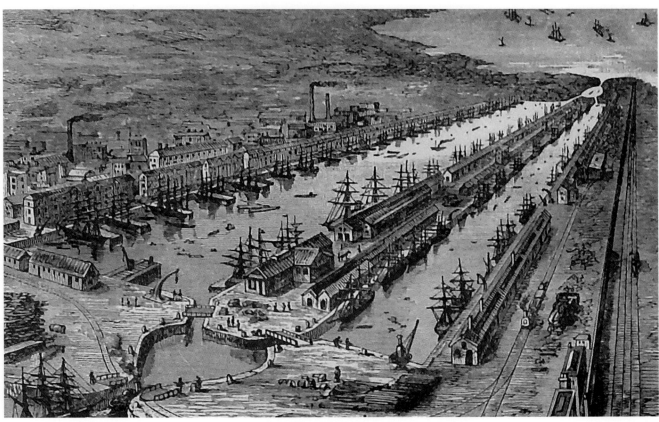

the north side of the river to the east of London Bridge.' There, 'between a slop-shop and a gin-shop, approached by a steep flight of steps leading down to a black gap like the mouth of a cave', he found the den he was looking for. This has been identified as being in Swan Lane, a closed-off side street in that vicinity.

Holmes makes another foray to the East End in 'The Adventure of the Six Napoleons' when he hurries to Stepney to talk to Gelder & Co., who were responsible for the manufacture of the busts in that story. (Gelder appears to be a Jewish name, in keeping with the many Jewish inhabitants of the vicinity, albeit the detective is met there by the manager who is 'a big, blond German'.) On the way, Holmes and Watson again get a scenic view of the contemporary capital as they dash 'through the fringe of fashionable London, hotel London, theatrical London, commercial London, and, finally, maritime London, till we came to a riverside city of a hundred thousand souls, where the tenement houses swelter and reek with the outcasts of Europe.'

The East End, described unsympathetically in this way, did not feature as much in the canon as the more salubrious West End. Being poorer and with considerably worse

housing conditions, it suffered a greater incidence of crime, which was often violent – from the Ratcliffe Highway murders at the start of the nineteenth century to the Jack the Ripper murders in Whitechapel at the end. (The Ripper atrocities took place in 1888, just as Conan Doyle was beginning to write his Holmes stories.)

One feature of the Ripper murders, in popular mythology as in real life, was the fog which swirled through London's dimly lit streets and alleys. It was pervasive in the Holmes stories, providing a suitable metaphor for the haziness that the detective sought to clarify. In 'The Adventure of the Bruce-Partington Plans' it is even helpfully dated. 'In the third week of November, in the year 1895, a dense yellow fog settled down upon London. From the Monday to the Thursday I doubt whether it was ever possible from our windows in Baker Street to see the loom of the opposite houses.'

This fog also came to represent Holmes's London, commemorated in a sonnet written by Vincent Starrett, a prominent member of the Baker Street Irregulars, the leading (American-based) 'scion' society of Holmes enthusiasts or 'Sherlockians', and often aired at their gatherings. It was written in 1942 at a time when the

Opposite The Thames Below London Bridge, *oil on canvas, by John Atkinson Grimshaw (1836–93).*

Left 'Jack the Ripper: the seventh horrible murder by the monster of the East End', from Police News, *17 November 1888.*

Below 'Over London by rail', *an illustration by Louis Auguste Gustave Doré (1832–83) from* London: A Pilgrimage *(1872).*

Above The Metropolitan
Underground Railway, *published
in* The Illustrated London
News, *27 December 1862.*

Opposite Paddington station
illustrated in Pictorial London
(c.1905).

English-speaking world was under threat from Nazi Germany (and when even the contemporary film version of the stories, starring Basil Rathbone, had been called into service as propaganda tools).

> Yellow fog swirls past the window-pane
> As night descends upon this fabled street:
> A lonely hansom splashes through the rain,
> The ghostly gas lamps fail at twenty feet.
> Here, though the world explode, these two survive,
> And it is always eighteen ninety-five.

This mood permeates Holmes stories, such as in *The Sign of Four*:

> It was a September evening and not yet seven o'clock, but the day had been a dreary one, and a dense drizzly fog lay low upon the great city. Mud-coloured clouds drooped sadly over the muddy streets. Down the Strand the lamps were but misty splotches of diffused light which threw a feeble circular glimmer upon the slimy pavement. The yellow glare from the shop-windows streamed out into the steamy, vaporous air and threw a murky, shifting radiance across the crowded thoroughfare. There was, to my mind, something eerie and ghostlike in the endless procession of faces which flitted across these narrow bars of light – sad faces and glad, haggard and merry.

Urban smells were strangely absent from the canon, where the most potent odour is tobacco. By most other accounts the capital reeked, partly from the excreta of the horses which still provided the most widespread form of transport, and partly from the sewers which flowed through the city. The situation had improved slightly following the Great Stink of 1858 (the year before Conan Doyle's birth), when stench from the River Thames, the main outlet for the sewers, pervaded the new House of Commons (still under construction after a convulsive fire in 1834) and forced even the legislators to take notice. The result was the construction of new larger sewers which channelled the polluted water further downstream to parts of the Thames estuary where it no longer affected urban populations. This involved reclaiming land from the river and covering them with embankments (the Chelsea, Albert and Victoria) which could then accommodate new roads as well as the tunnels for the new underground railway (later the District and Circle lines). Completed by 1870, this was a prime example of the vast municipal reconstruction projects which were being undertaken throughout the country. The Thames Embankment was the work of the great civil engineer Sir Joseph Bazalgette, to whom Conan Doyle's friend Percy Boulnois had once been apprenticed.

The underground railways or the Tube helped encourage mobility around the capital, working with the railways to bring passengers from the suburbs to earn their livings in the City and elsewhere. (The word 'commuter' was then only used, and sparingly, in an American context.) Like the banker Alexander Holder in 'The Adventure of the Beryl Coronet, visitors to Holmes in Baker Street often sometimes emerged from the underground station of that name, which was on the original Metropolitan Line from Paddington to Farringdon Street, dating from 1863. The carriages were initially steam-hauled and the tunnels 'cut and cover' (the roads had simply been dug up, the lines laid, and the road replaced, so they were close to the surface). Later, deeper shafts were bored, and the lines extended northwards into the Buckinghamshire countryside. At no stage was journeying on the underground a pleasant

experience. The American-born journalist R.D. Blumenfeld described a journey from Baker Street to Moorgate in 1887 as like his 'first experience of Hades', with the smoking passengers contributing to an atmosphere that was 'a mixture of sulphur, coal dust and foul fumes from the oil lamp above'.

Holmes needed to be as familiar with the underground railway system as with the streets above. This knowledge helped him make a crucial deduction in 'The Adventure of the Bruce-Partington Plans', written in 1908. He shows that the dead Arthur Cadogan West could not have been killed where he was found close to Aldgate station, since his body had been dumped on the roof of a Tube carriage as far away as Gloucester Road on the Metropolitan District Line, outside the house at 13 Caufield Gardens, inhabited by the notorious crook Hugo Oberstein. (This fictional address has been linked to nearby Cornwall Gardens.)

After lodging with Holmes, Dr Watson married and moved to a practice near Paddington station where, as noted in 'The Adventure of the Engineer's Thumb', his patients included several railway workers. Paddington was another of the original stations built in the capital, dating from 1838 as a terminus for the Great Western

Railway at Bishops Bridge Road; it was then rebuilt in a grander style sixteen years later by the engineer Isambard Kingdom Brunel on the nearby site it still occupies today. It provided one of the great arteries in and out of London, often used by Holmes on his journeys to investigate new cases. He meets Watson there before they board the train *en route* to Ross-on-Wye ('passing through the beautiful Stroud Valley, and over the broad gleaming Severn') before taking a carriage into the Herefordshire countryside to probe the Boscombe Valley mystery. Paddington is also the station of embarkation for Eyford, near Reading, in 'The Adventure of the Engineer's Thumb', for the fictional King's Pyland (two miles from Tavistock in Devon) in 'The Adventure of Silver Blaze', and for 'a small wayside station' in an unidentified town in a similar part of the country, Dartmoor, in *The Hound of the Baskervilles*. In 'The Adventure of Silver Blaze' Holmes and return to Victoria station from Winchester – a rare example of Conan Doyle, or maybe Watson on behalf of Sherlock Holmes getting his geography, and the railway network, wrong, for Waterloo would have been the terminus used on this journey. (In their defence, it has been argued that the pair could have changed trains at Clapham Junction to get to Victoria.)

Despite his prodigious memory, even Holmes occasionally had to resort to external sources of knowledge, such as the Encyclopaedia, almost certainly the *Encyclopaedia Britannica*, for which he 'shot out his long, thin arm' in 'The Adventure of the Priory School'. For information about places he was visiting outside London he relied on Ordnance Survey maps. (In *The Hound of the Baskervilles* he sends down for a 'very large scale' one from Stanford's, the specialist map shop in Covent Garden which still exists today, although on a different site.) And for corroboration about the times of trains' departures and their routes, Holmes relied on a printed resource: *Bradshaw's Guide*. Published in regular editions from 1839, this provided timetables for the fast-expanding railway services. Holmes would ask Watson to consult it, as when planning to travel to Winchester in 'The Adventure of the Copper Beeches'. '"Will you come with me?" asked Holmes, glancing up. "I should wish to." "Just look it up, then." "There is a train at half-past nine," said I, glancing over my Bradshaw. "It is due at Winchester at 11:30." "That will do very nicely."'

On this trip to what he calls the 'old English capital' of Winchester, Holmes startled his companion by revealing

a hitherto unknown aversion to the countryside which, he argued, harboured even more crime than the teeming capital. To the eager Watson, 'It was an ideal spring day, a light blue sky, flecked with little fleecy white clouds drifting across from west to east. The sun was shining very brightly, and yet there was an exhilarating nip in the air, which set an edge to a man's energy.'

But Holmes saw this rural environment in a very different manner. He told Watson. 'You look at these scattered houses, and you are impressed by their beauty. I look at them, and the only thought which comes to me is a feeling of their isolation and of the impunity with which crime may be committed there.' And when Watson expresses surprise at this, Holmes replied, 'They always fill me with a certain horror. It is my belief, Watson, founded upon my experience, that the lowest and vilest alleys in London do not present a more dreadful record of sin than does the smiling and beautiful countryside.' He added that the reason was obvious:

> The pressure of public opinion can do in the town what the law cannot accomplish. There is no lane so vile that the scream of a tortured child, or the thud of a drunkard's blow, does not beget sympathy and indignation among the neighbours, and then the whole machinery of justice is ever so close that a word of complaint can set it going, and there is but a step between the crime and the dock. But look at these lonely houses, each in its own fields, filled for the most part with poor ignorant folk who know little of the law. Think of the deeds of hellish cruelty, the hidden wickedness which may go on, year in, year out, in such places, and none the wiser.

This was a singular attitude to these bucolic surroundings, and one belied by Holmes' enthusiasm elsewhere for getting out of the city. He usually seemed happy to hop on a train and travel to some rural destination, such as Hereford in 'The Boscombe Valley Mystery'. And it was to the countryside that he chose to go when he stopped officially working. In 'The Adventure of the Lion's Mane', one of only two stories narrated by Holmes rather than Watson, the detective tells how he came to retire to a cottage on the Sussex Downs, in a place not far from the sea which has been identified as being near East Dean, outside Eastbourne. There he admitted that the main attraction of the place was its closeness to the soil. 'I had given myself up entirely to

Opposite Waterloo Bridge, Grey Weather *(1905), oil on canvas, by Claude Monet (1840–1926).*

Top The Railway Station *(1862), oil on canvas, by William Powell Frith (1819–1909).*

Above 'Holmes gave me a sketch of the events', Sidney Paget's illustration from The Memoirs of Sherlock Holmes *(1894).*

that soothing life of Nature for which I had so often yearned during the long years spent amid the gloom of London.'

Holmes did not often describe the fauna and flora outside London. But by the sea, close to his new house, he identified the venomous jellyfish *Cyanea capillata*, which had been responsible for the mysterious death of Fitzroy McPherson (the maths teacher at The Gables, the preparatory school run by his friend Harold Stackhurst) in 'The Adventure of the Lion's Mane'. Earlier, in *His Last Bow* he had expanded on his love of bees, the subject of one of his monographs, *Practical Handbook of Bee Culture, with Some Observations upon the Segregation of the Queen,* which he described to Watson as the fruit of his 'leisured ease'. He added, apropos the bees, 'Alone I did it. Behold the fruit of pensive nights and laborious days when I watched the little working gangs as once I watched the criminal world of London.' So, even in retirement in the countryside he maintained the focused curiosity which characterized the rest of his life.

Admittedly, most of the canonical descriptions of rural England came from Watson rather than Holmes. It was the Doctor who waxed lyrical about the Surrey heath around Farnham in 'The Adventure of the Solitary Cyclist'. He recalled his arrival there with his detective companion:

> A rainy night had been followed by a glorious morning, and the heath-covered countryside, with the glowing clumps of flowering gorse, seemed all the more beautiful to eyes which were weary of the duns and drabs and slate greys of London. Holmes and I walked along the broad, sandy road inhaling the fresh morning air and rejoicing in the music of the birds and the fresh breath of the spring. From a rise of the road on the shoulder of Crooksbury Hill, we could see the grim Hall bristling out from amidst the ancient oaks, which, old as they were, were still younger than the building which they surrounded.

This area was well known to Conan Doyle as he had lived in nearby Hindhead from 1897, having chosen the elevated position on the North Downs because of its suitability for his wife, Louise, who had been diagnosed with tuberculosis. He used it as a backdrop to his historical novel *Sir Nigel*

Opposite Illustration by Frederic Dorr Steele (1873–1944) for 'The Adventure of the Lion's Mane'.

Below Undershaw, near Hindhead in Surrey, where Conan Doyle lived from 1897–1907.

(1905–06) in the same way that his earlier *The White Company* (1891), about the Hundred Years' War, lovingly evoked the rural Hampshire that he used to visit when he was a GP in Southsea. He had particularly enjoyed the New Forest, which was where, after he married for a second time, he acquired a country cottage at Minstead, where the church was later the site of his grave.

The landscape most associated with Holmes is further west, on Dartmoor, in Devon, as featured in *The Hound of the Baskervilles*. Again, though lovingly described in the stories, the moor had an ambiguous appeal, as hinted at by Watson when he first arrived at Baskerville Hall. Having described the 'rolling pasture lands curved upward on either side of us, and old gabled houses peeped out from amid the thick green foliage,' he says, 'but behind the peaceful and sunlit countryside there rose ever, dark against the evening sky, the long, gloomy curve of the moor, broken by the jagged and sinister hills.' The fog had followed him there from London:

> Every minute that white woolly plain which covered one-half of the moor was drifting closer and closer to the house. Already the first thin wisps of it were curling across the golden square of the lighted

window. The farther wall of the orchard was already invisible, and the trees were standing out of a swirl of white vapour. As we watched it the fog-wreaths came crawling round both corners of the house and rolled slowly into one dense bank on which the upper floor and the roof floated like a strange ship upon a shadowy sea.

In another story, 'The Adventure of the Devil's Foot', published in 1910 and set further west in Cornwall, Watson points to a possible explanation for his friend's ambivalence towards the countryside. They are staying in a little whitewashed house, situated on a grassy headland, and overlooking 'the whole sinister semicircle of Mounts Bay, that old death trap of sailing vessels, with its fringe of black cliffs and surge-swept reefs on which innumerable seamen have met their end.' And on the other landward side, 'In every direction upon these moors there were traces of some vanished race which had passed utterly away, and left as its sole record strange monuments of stone, irregular mounds which contained the burned ashes of the dead, and curious earthworks which hinted at prehistoric strife.' Observing these details, Watson suggested, 'The glamour and mystery

of the place, with its sinister atmosphere of forgotten nations, appealed to the imagination of my friend, and he spent much of his time in long walks and solitary meditations upon the moor.' In other words, yet again, that Holmes could not be satisfied merely with the physical attractions of a place; he needed some stimulation, some intellectual input, to bring it alive. He had to be involved in some sort of quest.

Holmes did venture abroad, but usually without Watson, so he left little description of it. Famously he went to Switzerland where he ended up confronting his arch-enemy Professor Moriarty at the Reichenbach Falls in 'The Final Problem'. Apart from making a brief appearance in Montpellier in 'The Disappearance of Lady Frances Carfax' this journey is the only foreign sortie by the detective that is described in detail. It begins at Victoria station where the 'second first class carriage from the front' on the Continental Express has been reserved for him and Watson. However, to wrongfoot Moriarty, they do not proceed to Dover, but instead change trains at Canterbury and go to Newhaven, from where they cross the Channel to Dieppe. Holmes has spoken of continuing to Switzerland via Luxembourg and Basle [*sic*] but actually travels via Brussels, Strasbourg and Geneva, where they somehow find time to take a week off,

ambling along the River Rhône which rises in the Swiss Alps. Eventually they reach Meiringen, the village at the bottom of the falls, which are graphically described:

> The torrent, swollen by the melting snow, plunges into a tremendous abyss, from which the spray rolls up like the smoke from a burning house. The shaft into which the river hurls itself is an immense chasm, lined by glistening coal-black rock, and narrowing into a creaming, boiling pit of incalculable depth, which brims over and shoots the stream onward over its jagged lip.

Holmes's practice as a consulting detective clearly extends to Europe and further afield. In *The Sign of Four* he boasts to Watson that he has recently helped François de Villard of the French detective service and directed him to two parallel cases, one at Riga in 1857 and the other at St Louis in 1871. (He is typically sceptical about this colleague's credentials, stating that de Villard has 'all the Celtic power of quick intuition, but he is deficient in the wide range of exact knowledge which is essential to the higher developments of his art.') Watson tells us

Opposite The Reichenbach Falls, *watercolour on paper, by Samuel Jackson (1794–1869).*

Left 'The death of Sherlock Holmes', Sidney Paget's illustration for 'The Final Problem' (1893).

Kalif Abdullah †.

Above The Khalifa Abdallahi ibn
Muhammad (1846–99), whom
Holmes meets in Khartoum.

Opposite The German
bacteriologist Robert Koch
(1843–1910) in his laboratory.

in 'The Adventure of the Seven Clocks' that, in his
business capacity, Holmes has travelled as far as Odessa
(in the case of the Trepoff murder) and Trincomalee
(regarding the otherwise unspecified 'singular tragedy
of the Atkinson brothers'). At one stage in the spring
of 1887, after working for up to five days at a stretch,
and never less than fifteen hours a day, on the 'whole
question of the Netherland-Sumatra Company and of
the colossal schemes of Baron Maupertuis', Holmes falls
ill in the Hotel Dulong in Lyon and, as described in 'The
Adventure of the Reigate Squires', Watson rushes to
his sick-bed.

But there is no attempt to convey what it means to
visit these places. After his seemingly terminal experience
at the Reichenbach Falls, Holmes escapes to Asia,
spending two years in the Himalayas, including some
time in Lhasa. He returns via Persia, Arabia (managing,
like the explorer Richard Burton, to penetrate the
forbidden city of Mecca), and Khartoum, where he
meets the Khalifa and later conveys the fruits of their
conversation to the British Foreign Office. He reaches
home having spent some months researching coal-tar
derivatives in a laboratory in Montpellier in the south
of France. But, again, he offers no topographical details.
(His liaison with the British government points to
something often hinted at by Sherlockians – that Holmes
was closely involved with the British intelligence. Indeed,
his brother Mycroft is often described as a senior official
in, if not the head of, the then still rudimentary secret
services. Holmes's meeting with the Khalifa is helpful
in dating his travels, as the man who ruled Sudan in
a despotic manner following the death of the Mahdi,
himself died in November 1899.)

Conan Doyle was more forthcoming than Sherlock
Holmes about the many places he visited. His travels
started when, as a student in Edinburgh in 1880, he
spent nearly six months as a doctor on a whaling ship,
the 575-ton SS *Hope*, in the Arctic. He returned with a
knowledge of the treacherous ice packs of the frozen north
which he recalled in various articles and in a memorable
pre-Holmes story titled 'The Captain of the Pole Star'.
Strangely 'Auld Reekie' (and Scotland in general) did
not feature in the Holmes stories. Having been born
there of Irish stock, Conan Doyle simply transferred his
allegiances to England and focused his attentions as a
writer on London, the city which gave him his first break
in that profession.

After graduating, he ventured further afield, travelling down the west coast of Africa, again as the ship's doctor, in a trading vessel, the SS *Mayumba*. This helped develop his knowledge of a world outside Europe (he had already spent several months at a Jesuit educational establishment in Austria after leaving his own school, Stonyhurst College) and gave an enduringly global perspective to his outlook and works.

Typical of his desire to observe the world, Conan Doyle took up photography, a hobby which took him to picturesque parts of Scotland, Ireland and later England, where he ventured onto Dartmoor with a camera in his hand. He wrote up his experiences for the *British Journal of Photography*, which published his first sustained pieces of journalism, no doubt encouraging him to maintain his output of fiction; before Sherlock Holmes, he contributed to magazines such as the *Cornhill* and *Temple Bar*.

As part of his preparation for moving from Portsmouth to London in early 1891, he visited Berlin (in an unsuccessful attempt to engage with the famous bacteriologist Robert Koch) and Vienna (to pursue his studies into ophthalmology, the speciality he hoped would make his name and fortune in Harley Street). His interest in the eye only underlined the importance to him of looking at the world around him.

In the 1890s he developed a passion for skiing, first in Norway and then in Switzerland, where he regularly visited Davos with his family. He published articles on this pastime, leading observers to suggest he introduced skiing to the Alps. This was not true; it was already well-established as a means of getting across mountains. But he certainly helped to popularize it as a sport for the British. His occasional articles on skiing showed the importance to him of defining a sense of place (and being able to describe it). He described one of his ascents of the Swiss mountains, which started at half past four in the morning in the village of Frauenkirch: 'A great pale moon was shining in a violet sky, with such stars as can only be seen in the tropics or the higher Alps. At quarter past five we turned from the road, and began to plod up the hillsides, over alternate banks of last year's grass, and slopes of snow.'

He honed his prose about the spots he visited in his accounts of trips to the United States in 1894 and Egypt the following year. The latter journey was significant as he gave up his holiday with his wife and worked for

a while as a war correspondent, reporting on the conflict between Britain and followers of the nationalist Mahdi in the Sudan. He was able to write about an unusual environment – the desert – and about a different culture – Islam – both of which he found appealing. In one despatch to *The Westminster Gazette* he wrote,

> But the moon would fade, the east would lighten,
> red feathers of cloud would drift in a colourless
> sky, and then, within a few minutes, night would
> have changed to full day, the golden edge of the
> sun would be showing over the orange desert, and
> all our vague night-begotten sentiment would turn
> to practical questions of how far we had come and
> where we were to halt.

Drawing on these experiences, he published a novel in 1898 called *The Tragedy of the Korosko*, a fictional account of the kidnapping of a party of tourists by a band of Mahdist 'dervishes'. This book has a claim to be the first in English literature to deal with Islamic fundamentalism. It was later turned into a play, *The Fires of Fate* (1909).

By then he was entering middle age and had remarried, following the death of his first wife Louise in 1906. Over the next few years, he took his new spouse Jean on trips to Europe, North Africa, the Middle East and North America, which they visited together in 1914, just before the First World War. After reflecting in articles for the *Cornhill Magazine*, later collected in his book *Western Wanderings* (1915), on how much New York had changed since his previous visit twenty years earlier, he particularly enjoyed crossing Canada on the Canadian Pacific Railway. Having travelled as far as the Rocky Mountains, he and Jean spent time in the newly created Jasper National Park in Alberta which he loved and regarded as a model of conservation practice:

> The park is not yet as full of wild creatures
> as it will be after a few years of preservation.
> The Indians who lived in this part rounded up
> everything that they could before moving to
> their reservation. But even now, the bear
> lumbers through the brushwood, the eagle soars
> above the lake, the timber wolf still skulks in the
> night, and the deer graze in the valleys. Above,
> near the snowline, the wild goat is not uncommon,

while at a lower altitude are found the mountain sheep. On the last day of our visit the rare cinnamon bear exposed his yellow coat upon a clearing humoured head looking at me from over a dead trunk, and I thanked the kindly Canadian law which has given him a place of sanctuary. What a bloodthirsty baboon man must appear to the lower animals! If any superhuman demon treated us exactly as we treat the pheasants, we should begin to reconsider our views as to what is sport.

As an occasional rhymester (with three books of poetry to his name) he took to verse to describe his side-visit to the Athabasca Trail, a former portage route 100 miles (160 kilometres) long that linked Edmonton and Athabasca, also in Alberta. A few lines convey his delight:

> I shall hear her mighty rivers where the waters
> foam and tear;
> I shall smell her virgin uplands with their balsam
> laden air;
> And in dreams I shall be riding down the
> winding wooded vale
> With the packer and the pack-horse on the
> Athabasca trail.

However, he had now become an unapologetic mouthpiece for the Empire. His account of his journey through Canada in *Western Wanderings* is full of well-meaning, if patronizing, admiration for the pioneers who had opened the prairies to efficient farming and development. The Canadian Pacific Railway, which had sponsored his trip, is often praised for its role in driving this process forward. He later adopted the same condescending tone in his writing about Australia in *Wanderings of a Spiritualist* (1921). He only seemed content if economic advances could be seen to be bolstering the imperial project.

By then he had met and clearly idolized some of the great explorers of the Edwardian age, including the Commanders Robert Peary and Ernest Shackleton who had been to the Arctic and Antarctic. In a speech to the Royal Societies Club in London in 1910, he did, however, blame Peary, who claimed to have reached the North Pole the previous year, for taking some of the magic out of travel. As reported in *The Times*, Conan Doyle said:

Opposite An illustration from Conan Doyle's 1898 novel The Tragedy of the Korosko.

Above The Connaught Tunnel in the Selkirk Mountains on the Canadian Pacific Railway, an illustration from Railways of Today *(c.1933).*

There had been a time when the world was full of blank spaces, and in which a man of imagination might be able to give free scope to his fancy. But owing to the ill-directed energy of their guest and other gentlemen of similar tendencies these spaces were rapidly being filled up and the question was where the romance writer was to turn when he wanted to draw any vague and not too clearly-defined region.

Such matters were in his mind because in 1912 he wrote his 'wild boys' book' *The Lost World*, which is largely based in the jungles of South America, a continent he had never visited, but nevertheless managed to describe vividly, having obtained information on from Roger Casement, the Irish-born British diplomat whom he had befriended through their attempts to expose atrocities in the Congo.

After the First World War, Conan Doyle continued to chalk up the miles, going to India, Australia and Africa, with further voyages to North America. But he had now embraced spiritualism and had embarked on a different type of journey – seeking contact with the spirits of people who had died. He was often derided for his deeply held beliefs, but on one level he hadn't given up exploring new frontiers. Like Holmes, he ended his days in Sussex, underlining once again the close parallels between the lives of the author and his creation.

Below Conan Doyle and his family on a picnic in Jasper Park in Alberta, Canada, in 1923.

BRITAIN AND
THE WIDER WORLD

Dr John Watson was being disingenuous, ignorant or perhaps wilfully obfuscatory when, early in *A Study in Scarlet*, he described his new friend Sherlock Holmes as having no (or only a feeble) knowledge of politics.

It is true that Holmes followed no obvious political party. But there is little doubt about his general orientation. He was a liberal imperialist, like the man who created him: Arthur Conan Doyle. And liberal in this context doesn't mean radical. It suggests someone fair and open-minded, opposed to exploitation and oppression, but generally conservative in his world view. Indeed – as indicated by his habit of firing bullets into the wall of his lodgings in Baker Street to mark out the initials V.R., in honour of his Queen Victoria – he was very much a monarchist.

At the time, in the last couple of decades of the nineteenth century, there were two main political affiliations in Britain – the Conservatives and the Liberals, the first long-dominated by Benjamin Disraeli (Lord Beaconsfield from 1876), and the latter by William Gladstone. In addition, a significant rump of Irish MPs fought under the rubric of the Irish Parliamentary Party, and, by the end of the 1880s, the voice of the working

classes was beginning to be heard in the Social Democratic Federation, Socialist League and, from 1895, the Independent Labour Party. To complicate matters, there was a split in the Liberal Party in 1886 over Gladstone's proposal to grant Home Rule to Ireland. Many supporters (some of them MPs, but also those outside parliament, such as Conan Doyle) left the Liberals and aligned themselves with the Conservatives (or Tories).

Conan Doyle hadn't taken much of an interest in politics while he was studying medicine in Edinburgh. But, from 1882, when he moved to Portsmouth as a GP, he gradually involved himself in local issues and, by extension, in the wider world of politics.

The first major subject on which he publicly took a stance was Irish Home Rule. His Irish roots were partly responsible. On his mother's side, the Foleys were a dynasty of hearty, mainly Protestant yeomen with substantial property holdings around Lismore in County Wexford, where his great-grandfather Thomas Foley had been the Duke of Devonshire's agent. As a result, the family was linked with the Anglo-Irish ascendancy, and took pride in the exploits of so-called 'Black Tom' Foley and his son Patrick, who killed a member of the Whiteboys (a secret

party of agrarian activists that flourished in the late eighteenth century). Conan Doyle's father's family was more solidly Catholic, with antecedents in the tailoring business in Dublin.

Since Conan Doyle's mother was mainly responsible for his upbringing, his childhood in Edinburgh was dominated by her conservative views, which were strongly opposed to any demonstration of Irish nationalism or Fenianism. A formative experience for him, aged seven, was accompanying her on a visit to some relations in Ireland and having to cower in a loft to escape from an abusive Fenian raiding party. This may well have been in 1867, when the Fenians carried out the Clerkenwell bombings in London, designed to free some of their members from prison. Twelve people had been killed and 120 injured in what *The Times* described as 'a crime of unrivalled atrocity'. As was clear from later works, he retained a deep distaste for the Fenians (depicted as the Molly Maguires in *The Valley of Fear*, for example). He saw such agitators as disruptive of the social good and consequently supported a firm sense of law and order.

The revival of the Fenian bombing campaign in Britain from 1881–5 led the Prime Minister, William

Gladstone, to seek an end to the intractable disputes over Britain's relationship with her Irish neighbour by publishing what became known as the First Irish Home Bill in April 1886 (more or less exactly when Conan Doyle was putting the finishing touches to *A Study in Scarlet*). But this piece of legislation was defeated when debated in the House of Commons on 8 June, precipitating a general election in July. This encouraged a significant faction in the Liberal Party, which opposed Home Rule, to defect and establish the new Liberal Unionist Party, which allied itself to the Conservatives, who, with this enhanced backing, duly won the election.

As he had now completed his book, Conan Doyle seized on this issue to demonstrate his support for this new party. On 6 July he wrote to the Portsmouth's *Evening News* declaring that, although he was 'a man holding liberal opinions on many of the leading issues of the day', he intended to vote for the Liberal Unionists. The main reason he gave was that, since 1881, Ireland had been torn apart by 'a long succession of crimes against life and property'. But 'these murders and maimings' had not been condemned by the existing Irish parliamentary party, which he feared would prejudice a cherished political goal

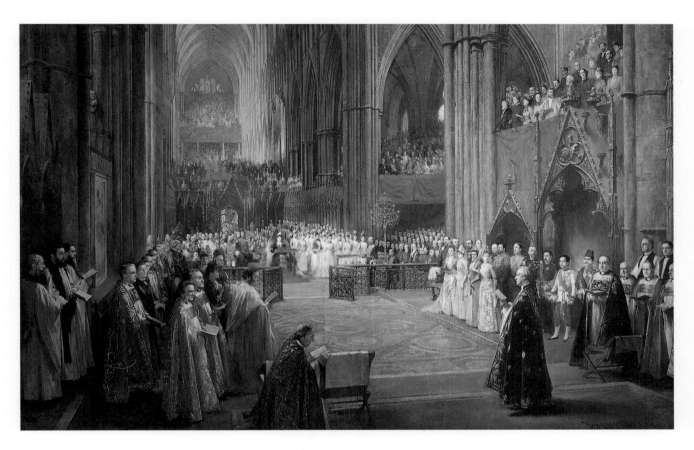

of his – the establishment of 'a grand scheme of Imperial
Federation' centred on Westminster. 'Any exceptional Irish
legislation of the nature proposed would hamper this just
and symmetrical design'.

Having been elected vice chairman of the local Liberal
Unionists, he found himself having to give an off-the-cuff
speech to a crowd of 3,000 people when the main speaker,
the new party's local candidate General Sir William
Crossman, had been delayed. 'It was one of the tight
corners of my life,' Conan Doyle later recalled. 'I hardly
knew myself what I said, but the Irish part of me came
to my aid and supplied me with a torrent of more or less
incoherent words and similes which roused the audience
greatly, though it read to me afterward more like a comic
stump speech than a serious effort.'

Not long afterwards he was again in action when
Arthur Balfour, a leading Conservative Unionist (and
nephew of the new party leader Lord Salisbury), came to
Portsmouth to speak against Gladstone. When the fair-
minded Conan Doyle stepped in to stop a heckler shouting
abuse at the visitor, he was knocked down. Crossman and
the official Conservative candidate, Sir Samuel Wilson,
were returned to parliament on this occasion, but the

overall result across the nation was indecisive, leading to a minority Conservative government which could only function with help from the Liberal Unionists. This unsatisfactory outcome changed when a further election the following year confirmed a majority Conservative administration under Salisbury, which established the political mood for most of the remainder of the century – unashamedly imperialistic in foreign affairs, mildly reformist, ever aware of the emerging Labour Party, at home. This would be the template for the rest of Conan Doyle's public life.

Sherlock Holmes was not so different. As much as he can be described as anything, he was socially liberal, a believer in incremental progress, along the lines of his creator. In 'The Adventure of the Naval Treaty' published in 1893, he shows genuine enthusiasm when he looks out from a train and alights on one of the Board Schools introduced in the Liberal government Elementary Education Act of 1870 to bring free education to children between five and twelve. 'Lighthouses, my boy!' he remarks to Watson. 'Beacons of the future! Capsules, with hundreds of bright little seeds in each, out of which will spring the wiser, better England of the future.'

Holmes has little enthusiasm for official Conservatism as a political creed if his unflattering observation of his client John Scott Eccles in 'The Adventure of Wisteria Lodge' is anything to go by. 'His life history was written in his heavy features and pompous manner. From his spats to his gold-rimmed spectacles he was a Conservative, a churchman, a good citizen, orthodox and conventional to the last degree.'

But his stories reflect little of the parliamentary discourse of the time. They are political only in the way they firmly reflect and uphold the established social order. The great detective acts for royalty and is at home with the hierarchical structure of English society, particularly when visiting the countryside. The great unwashed may feature peripherally, but he shows scant sympathy for their political aspirations.

However, Holmes does his best to be even-handed whenever politics does intrude, as is clear from his reaction to newspaper reports of the so-called 'Brixton Mystery', the murder of Enoch Drebber at the centre of *A Study in Scarlet*. According to this story, the press coverage was generally xenophobic, suggesting the atrocity had been committed by a foreigner. The *Daily Telegraph* declared,

'The German name of the victim, the absence of all other motive, and the sinister inscription on the wall, all pointed to its perpetration by political refugees and revolutionists.' But Holmes aimed for some balance with his record of the contrasting views of two further newspapers. *The Standard* adopted the line that 'lawless outrages of the sort usually occurred under a Liberal administration. They arose from the unsettling of the minds of the masses, and the consequent weakening of all authority.' Meanwhile *The Daily News* had no doubt that the crime had a political motive, observing, 'The despotism and hatred of Liberalism which animated the Continental governments had the effect of driving to our shores a number of men who might have made excellent citizens were they not soured by the recollection of all that they had undergone.' These last two comments clearly attempted to give two sides of the picture – the first equating lawlessness with Liberal administrations, the second suggesting that Liberalism was an attractive creed, despised by despots.

Impartiality is important for Holmes. When a politician does enter the frame, he is not identified by party. For example, when, somewhat unusually in 'The Adventure of the Second Stain', Holmes is visited in Baker Street by the Prime Minister, Lord Bellinger ('austere, high-nosed, eagle-eyed, and dominant') and the Secretary for European Affairs, the Right Honourable Trelawney Hope, there is no indication of their political party. However, Bellinger has often been taken to represent Lord Salisbury, the Prime Minister in 1888, the year in which the case apparently took place.

As someone without obvious party affiliation, Holmes comes across as a decent fellow, with no truck with authoritarianism or manifest injustice. If anything, he is a bit of an anarchist, prepared on occasions to take the law into his own hands and free individuals who have transgressed. One example is the way he declines to turn over the sailor Captain Croker to the police in 'The Adventure of Abbey Grange'. Holmes had been called to the house in Chislehurst in Kent where the elderly and abusive Sir Eustace Brackenstall had been murdered, apparently by thieving intruders. Holmes works out that the killer is probably Croker, who had been Lady Brackenstall's lover. However, he learns from a maid that Croker only acted in self-defence when Brackenstall discovered him with his wife. Holmes is struck by his evident love for the woman, and decides not to involve the local constabulary. He tells Croker:

This is a very serious matter, though I am willing to admit that you acted under the most extreme provocation to which any man could be subjected. I am not sure that in defence of your own life your action will not be pronounced legitimate. However, that is for a British jury to decide. Meanwhile I have so much sympathy for you that, if you choose to disappear in the next 24 hours, I will promise you that no one will hinder you.

Similarly, he takes no action against James Ryder, who stole the Blue Carbuncle in the story of that name. This is partly because it is Christmas, the season of forgiveness. But he also states clearly, 'I am not retained by the police to supply their deficiencies.' He admits he could be committing a felony, but argues he might also be saving a soul. 'This fellow will not go wrong again; he is too terribly frightened. Send him to jail now, and you make him a jail-bird for life.' A modern legal reformer could not have put it better.

Two other examples of Holmes playing God and disregarding the letter of the law occur in 'The Adventure of the Devil's Foot' and 'The Adventure of Charles Augustus Milverton'. In the former, Holmes lets Leon Sterndale off the hook for the unlikely reason that he admires the strength of the explorer's love for the murdered Brenda Tregennis. The latter case is more complex, with Holmes – to Watson's horror – getting engaged to a maid in order to gain access to Milverton's house, and then burning incriminatory papers in a blackmail case. He is apprehended and escapes, but later refuses to help Inspector Lestrade of Scotland Yard on the case because his 'sympathies' are with the criminals (which, of course, are himself and Watson). According to the American Sherlockian scholar Robert Keith Leavitt, in the sixty stories in the canon, there are thirty-seven felonies where the criminal was known to Holmes, and in fourteen of these the detective takes the law into his own hands and frees the guilty person.

Holmes's own version of justice clearly reflects the reforming aspirations of his creator. Even in Portsmouth in June 1887 Conan Doyle was writing to both the local *Evening News* and the *Hampshire County Times* advocating for smallpox vaccination, giving as a reference a publication of the National Health Society, which had been founded by the Anglo-American social activist Elizabeth Blackwell to promote women in the medical profession. This latter cause was important to him; *Round the Red Lamp*, his 1894 collection of (mainly) medical stories, included 'The Doctors

"'HAVE MERCY! HE SHRIEKED.'"

Opposite Holmes and Watson meet the Prime Minister (Lord Bellinger) and the Secretary for European Affairs (the Rt Hon. Trelawney Hope) in Granada TV's The Return of Sherlock Holmes: The Second Stain *(1986).*

Above 'Have mercy! he shrieked', an 1892 illustration by Sidney Paget for 'The Adventure of the Blue Carbuncle'.

of Hoyland', which explored how a bigoted doctor's attitude changes from aversion to admiration and even love for a new medical colleague in a nearby village after discovering she is a woman. Separately, in 1898, he published in *The Strand Magazine* 'The Story of the Black Doctor' which told how a non-white GP came to be accepted in a Lancashire hamlet. He turns out to be Argentinian, from an old Spanish family, but the point is about the integration of a visibly foreign man into the community.

After becoming a household name, Conan Doyle increasingly used his reputation to push for changes on public issues. In 1911 he became president of the Divorce Law Reform Union, a subject close to his heart as he had been unable to leave his first wife, Louise, after falling in love with another woman, Jean Leckie. In 1909 he wrote a polemical book *The Crime of the Congo* in support of the Congo Reform Association, which had been set up to lobby against the evils of the rubber plantations owned by the Belgian King Leopold II in that vast area of Africa. He himself often turned detective and tried to right obvious injustices, such as the conviction of the half-Indian solicitor George Edalji for maiming horses in Staffordshire in 1903. He also used his influence to publicize the case of Oscar

Slater, a dealer in precious stones, who in 1909 was accused of robbing and killing an eighty-three-year-old spinster in Glasgow.

Conan Doyle's concerns about the Congo show his political interests extending beyond England, as did those of Sherlock Holmes, whose exploits so often reflected the concerns of his creator. Four main areas are worth exploring: Ireland, the United States, the British Empire and Europe.

Ireland has already been touched on. It was a theme which continued to play through Conan Doyle's work. Having identified himself as a Liberal Unionist in the mid-1880s, he maintained this affiliation during the golden years of Conservative ascendancy under Lord Salisbury over the following decade. When chairing a dinner of the Irish Literary Society in the Café Monico in London's Regent Street in June 1897, he antagonized many of the attendees by insisting that the loyal toast be drunk. He even stood as a Liberal Unionist candidate in two elections – once in his hometown of Edinburgh Central in the 'khaki' or wartime election of October 1900 and then again in the Scottish Border Burghs (or Boroughs) in 1905. On both occasions he was defeated.

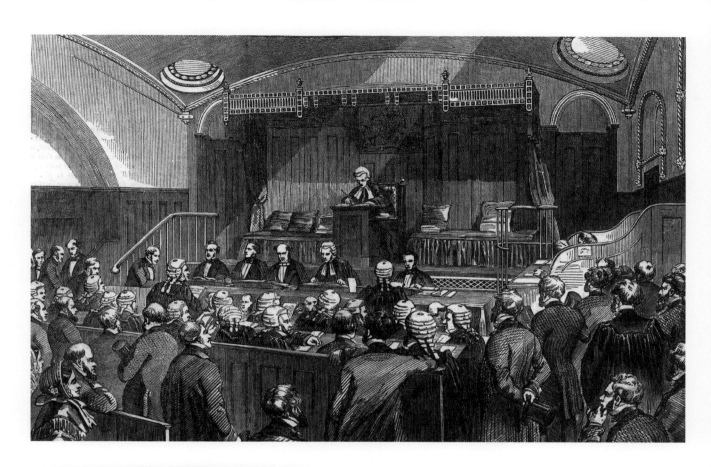

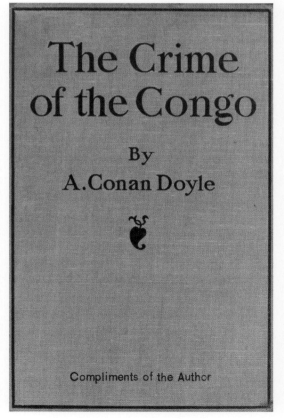

Opposite An illustration showing a doctor in England vaccinating children against smallpox, published in Harper's Weekly *magazine, 1871.*

Above Illustration of the Court for Divorce and Matrimonial Causes in Westminster Hall, published in The Ilustrated London News, *1858.*

Left Advance copy (1909) of Conan Doyle's The Crime of the Congo.

By this time, in the first decade of the new century, a backlash against the Boer War and conservatism had set in. This led to a decade of Liberal governments under Henry Campbell-Bannerman and Herbert Asquith, which reformed the House of Lords and introduced the People's Budget of 1909–10 with its radical provisions of national insurance and unemployment pay. Not content with that, the Liberals attempted, in 1913, to reintroduce the cherished Gladstonian policy of Home Rule for Ireland. But the implementation was a disaster, with the Northern Irish in Ulster refusing to participate and British troops stationed in the Curragh Camp within Ireland mutinying in 1914, just before the start of the First World War. The subsequent secessionist Easter Rising in Ireland of 1916 failed, but British presence thereafter was problematic and repressive, leading to the establishment of the Irish Free State in 1922.

Significantly, Conan Doyle shifted his attitude on this matter in the years leading up to the First World War when, partly as a result of his friendship with Roger Casement (the Dublin-born former British diplomat who became a campaigner for Irish independence), he belatedly came to support the policy of Home Rule. But he saw the solution to the underlying problem rather differently from Casement, who wanted and was prepared to fight for full Irish independence. Conan Doyle preferred Ireland to remain a member of a new federation of nations professing allegiance to the British crown. This point of view did not stop him lobbying for a commutation of the death sentence handed out to Casement for treason for his active support of the rebels in the 1916 uprising.

And while he softened in his views on Home Rule, he never overcame his antipathy towards Fenianism, the violent face of Irish republicanism – an obsession that re-emerged in his novel *The Valley of Fear*, published in 1915. As with *A Study in Scarlet*, this was a murder investigation with dark antecedents in the United States; members of a secret society, the Scowrers, travel from the United States to England to kill a former Pinkerton's detective, who had infiltrated and exposed them. The Scowrers were based on the Molly Maguires, a covert group of activists with links to the Fenians, who waged violent campaigns against mine owners in the Irish-dominated coal industry in Pennsylvania.

Perhaps this old prejudice led to the creation of Holmes's Irish arch-rival, Professor James Moriarty. Moriarty took his surname from two Irish brothers who had been at Stonyhurst College with Conan Doyle.

Opposite This 'Home Rule Map of Ireland' (1893) contains the complete text of the First Home Rule Bill and an analysis of the 1892 General Election.

Above The 1922 US film Sherlock Holmes *was released in the UK as* Moriarty.

Above Conan Doyle met Henry Highland Garnet (1815–82), the African-American minister and abolitionist in 1881.

Opposite Oliver Wendell Holmes (1809–94), after whom Conan Doyle's detective was named.

Being Roman Catholic and near the Irish sea, the school had many Irish pupils, including a Patrick Sherlock who arrived there in the same term as Holmes's creator.

For all this, Conan Doyle was often sympathetic towards Ireland and its inhabitants in his fiction. In an early non-Sherlockian story 'That Little Square Box' (published in *London Society* in December 1881), he satirized the knee-jerk reaction linking the Irish with terrorism (in this case, a box thought to contain dynamite was found to be transporting racing pigeons). In 'The Green Flag' (published more than a decade later in June 1893 in *Pall Mall Magazine*), Irish soldiers from a regiment tainted by Fenianism rally to the British Imperial cause they despise when confronted by a horde of dervishes in the Sudan.

Conan Doyle's personal approach to the United States was less affected by family ties, and therefore generally more straightforward. His love of the country had started as a child when he had devoured colourful romances of the American Wild West. He later championed the American historian Francis Packman, whose seven-volume *France and England in North America* (1865–92) he adopted as a source book for his 1893 historical novel *The Refugees: A Tale of Two Continents* about Huguenot Protestants forced to flee Catholic France and find shelter in the United States.

Conan Doyle's romantic view of North America took a new turn after he met Henry Highland Garnet, a dignified Black American diplomat, on the SS *Mayumba*, where he was working as a temporary ship's doctor in 1881 shortly after he left Edinburgh University. Garnet, a campaigning abolitionist who was bound for a job as United States consul in Liberia, impressed the eager young medical graduate with the breadth of his learning. Garnet also happened to be a friend of Oliver Wendell Holmes, the influential Boston-based doctor and essayist who gave his name to Conan Doyle's fictional detective.

Conan Doyle's attitude was not so rosy that he could ignore the periodic hiccups which bedevilled Anglo-US relations, however. The Monroe Doctrine, Washington's declaration of its hegemony over the Americas in 1821, antagonized many in Whitehall, and Britain's divided sympathies in the bloody American Civil War (1861–5) still had repercussions.

Conan Doyle was well aware that the United States had a violent and unpredictable history, and, as an author, he used this fact to heighten the tension in his Sherlock Holmes tales, starting with the very first, *A Study in Scarlet*, in 1887. As well as introducing Holmes's detective skills

in London, this investigative saga was fleshed out with a back story set in the United States in 1847. This involved a father and daughter, John and Lucy Ferrier, who are lost in the Western Desert in Utah; they are rescued by members of the Church of the Latter Day Saints, or Mormons, who had settled in Salt Lake City (the capital of that state) that very year, after a gruelling cross-country trek from New York. Ferrier agrees to follow their religion, but balks at their practice of polygamy. This causes problems when Lucy falls in love with a non-Mormon, Jefferson Hope, but is told she must get married within the church – to either Enoch Drebber or Joseph Stangerson, sons of members of the ruling Council of Four. When Lucy tries to escape, her father is killed and she dies soon afterwards, having been forced to marry Drebber. Hope swears to avenge her death, even if this means going to London to tackle Drebber and Stangerson, who have decamped there after an internal Mormon feud. Hope eventually finds them and exacts his bloody revenge, allowing Holmes to show his talents as a sleuth and solve the case.

The story makes clear that neither the physical environment nor the native inhabitants of America were always benign. It was a wild country, fraught with danger and, unlike well-governed Britain, subject to whims and lawlessness that could give rise to an unregulated cult, such as the Mormons, or to out-and-out criminals, such as John Garrideb. In 'The Adventure of the Three Garridebs', John Winter (who has three pseudonyms, John Garrideb, Morecroft and Killer Evans) crosses the Atlantic in 1893 and promptly kills Rodger Prescott, a notorious forger from Chicago. As Holmes discovers, Winter had served time in the United States for the murder of three men.

Another story of murderous vengeance crossing the Atlantic was 'The Five Orange Pips'. It told how, after flourishing as a planter in Florida, John Openshaw's Uncle Elias signed up to the Confederate Army, rising to the rank of colonel in the Civil War. He later joined the racist Ku Klux Klan which, in its initial post-conflict incarnation, operated as a terrorist organization in the southern United States. Then 'about 1869 or 1870', according to the story, 'he came back to Europe and took a small estate in Sussex, near Horsham', where he lived as an often-drunken recluse. But he had fallen foul of the Klan, whose members followed and later assassinated him in a manner ingeniously unravelled by Holmes.

'The Five Orange Pips' highlighted something of a trope in the Holmes stories – the United States as a place where people achieved something, often wealth, before coming to Britain to establish a new life in the countryside. One example was John Douglas who, after making his fortune in America in *The Valley of Fear*, decamped to what he mistakenly hoped was the rural tranquillity of Birlstone in Sussex. Slightly different was Elsie Patrick, who escaped her Chicago crime-boss father to marry Hilton Cubitt and live at Riding Thorpe Manor in Norfolk where, as Cubitt himself put it in 'The Adventure of the Dancing Men', his people had been 'for a matter of five centuries, and there is no better known family in the County of Norfolk.' In 'The Adventure of the Noble Bachelor', the marriage of Lord St Simon (son of a former British Foreign Minister with Plantagenet and Tudor blood in his line) to Miss Hatty Doran ('fascinating' daughter of a California millionaire) is rudely interrupted when her past comes back to haunt her. Rather more innocuously, even Irene Adler, the woman who threatened to blackmail the King of Bohemia in *A Study in Scarlet*, had been born in New Jersey before embarking on a career as an opera singer, which took her to Warsaw and elsewhere.

Opposite The Western Desert of Utah, which features in a flash-back in the first Sherlock Holmes story, A Study in Scarlet.

Below 'I will wish you all a very good night', an 1892 illustration by Sidney Paget for 'The Adventure of the Noble Bachelor'.

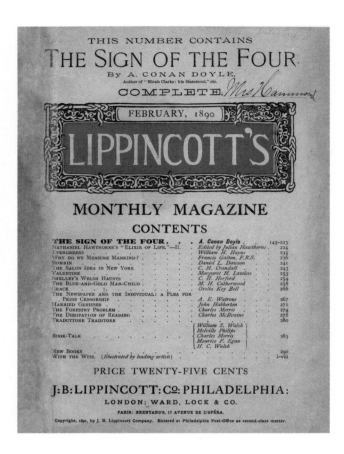

Above 'The Sign of the Four' published in the US edition of Lippincott's Monthly Magazine *(1890).*

Opposite Waterloo Bridge, Looking East, *oil on canvas, by John Atkinson Grimshaw (1836–93).*

In all, fifteen of the stories, including three of the novels, involved American characters. This focus reflected Conan Doyle's continuing personal warmth towards the United States. He may well have felt indebted to the Philadelphia publisher J.M. Stoddart for commissioning *The Sign of Four* in 1889. His trans-Atlantic readers subsequently became an important, if not the largest, market for his writings. Two years later, he indicated an important factor in his attitude when he wrote in the epigraph to his novel *The White Company*:

> To the hope of the future
> The reunion of the English-speaking races
> This little chronicle of our common ancestry
>   is inscribed.

He expanded on this in the words of Francis Hay Moulton, the sometime gold prospector who threatens to upset the happily married future of the 'noble bachelor' in the Holmes story of that name, published the following year in April 1892. This included the immortal lines:

> It is always a joy to meet an American, Mr Moulton, for I am one of those who believes that the folly of a monarch and the blundering of a minister in far-gone years will not prevent our children from being some day citizens of the same world-wide country under a flag which shall be a quartering of the Union Jack with the Stars and Stripes.

Conan Doyle had by this time been thinking deeply about Britain's place in the world and how it might collaborate with the United States to establish a federation of English-speaking nations. In December 1892 he wrote to *The Times* from the aptly named Reform Club with a novel suggestion. Germany had refused to let any of its military bands play at the Chicago Exhibition. He suggested that a British band should go instead. 'It appears to me … to be just one of those occasions for cementing international friendship which seldom present themselves and which are too valuable to neglect.' He underlined what he had in mind in a letter to the *Daily Chronicle* the following March:

> All plans for the future of our race which omit the United States are as vain as the planning of an arch without the keystone. No difference of

government or manners can alter the fact that the largest collection of people of Anglo-Celtic descent in the world is to be found from the other side of the Atlantic. If, therefore, the race is destined (as I firmly believe that it is) to become more homogeneous in the future, it is certainly not only that this vast block of people must be regarded as a factor in the problem, but that their wishes will have a great deal to do with its solution.

And he went on to suggest, not for the first time, that the English-speaking peoples should be 'organized into a union of Commonwealths which shall be founded upon no artificial treaty, but upon the permanent basis of common blood, and in the main of common traditions.'

This affection for the United States only deepened after his first trip there, a lecture tour, in 1894. It was now reinforced by his perception that America's support would be vital if he were to realize this particular dream of an English-speaking federation. His mission in this respect wasn't secret. When he considered crossing the Atlantic again the following year, his fellow author, Rudyard

Kipling (whom he had visited in his then home in Vermont), wrote of him to a friend, 'He's great on binding America and England more closely together.'

Conan Doyle did not, in fact, return to the United States in 1895 (his wife had been diagnosed with tuberculosis and he needed to take her to Egypt to benefit from the winter sun), but his idea of a worldwide Anglo-Saxon partnership was now firmly on the political agenda. It had been given a boost by Cecil Rhodes, the mining magnate whose ambitions for British control over Africa had frequently provoked the Boer Republic, leading to the South African (or Boer) War of 1899. Conan Doyle wanted to fight in this distant conflict, but he was too old and had to make do with serving briefly in a hospital in his old profession as a doctor. He subsequently wrote a history of the war, as well as a polemic in its defence – *The War in South Africa: Its Cause and Conduct* – published in 1902, which led to him being awarded a knighthood.

By then, Conan Doyle's fervour for Anglo-US collaboration on global issues had waned. He was more exercised by the threat of German expansionism in Europe. And his approach to the United States was more driven by his bank balance than by grand global concepts. America

Above Boer War Skirmish, *gouache on paper, by James Edwin McConnell (1903–95).*

Opposite above Sherlock Holmes *at the Reichenbach Falls, on the cover of* Collier's *magazine, 26 September 1903.*

Opposite below A New York poster *advertising William Gillette's first stage portrayal of the detective (c.1900).*

had developed into the most lucrative market for his work. It was a substantial offer from *Collier's* magazine in New York which persuaded him, after a ten-year lay-off, to resurrect Sherlock Holmes from his apparent Swiss-mountain grave in 'The Adventure of the Empty House' in October 1903. The American actor, William Gillette, fanned the detective's fame by bringing his exploits to the stage in Buffalo and New York in late 1899. Gillette's theatrical renditions of Sherlock Holmes were hugely successful, and film versions of the canon followed. When Conan Doyle next visited the United States, in 1914, he went mainly as a tourist, introducing his new wife Jean to the Continent. And the same was true of subsequent trans-Atlantic sorties in 1922 and 1923, when his travels had a new focus – spreading the message of spiritualism.

Another reason why Conan Doyle cooled towards America politically was that, after the Boer War, a narrower vision of the future of Britain and her Empire had come to dominate his worldview. A variation on Anglo-Saxonism underlay the new economic policy of protectionism advocated by the British Conservative (formerly Radical) politician Joseph Chamberlain in the late 1890s. But he wanted a system of imperial preference, which granted favourable tariffs only to British dominions and colonies. The United States was not part of it.

Conan Doyle had initially been lukewarm towards protectionism, if Holmes's attitude in *The Hound of the Baskervilles* (written in 1901 and published the following year) is anything to go by. In this story, the detective quotes a fictional newspaper article to Watson:

> You may be cajoled into imagining that your own special trade or your own industry will be encouraged by a protective tariff, but it stands to reason that such legislation must in the long run keep away wealth from the country, diminish the value of our imports, and lower the general conditions of life in this island.

And then, 'in high glee, rubbing his hands together with satisfaction', he asks Watson's opinion, 'Don't you think that is an admirable sentiment?'

By the time he fought the 1905 general election as a Unionist candidate in the Border Burghs his views had clearly changed. He had adopted protectionism wholeheartedly, imagining, as he recorded in *Memories and Adventures*, that since the small towns of that constituency (Hawick, Galashiels and Selkirk) were all engaged in the wool trade, which was hard hit by German competition, they would rally to this cause. But his hopes were misplaced, and for the second time he was not elected.

At the same time, Conan Doyle's attitude to the Empire had evolved. Indeed, the very concept had changed. When he went to work in Southsea in 1882, people still talked about the colonies, rather than the Empire. That was how the hordes of former servicemen and administrators who retired there would have regarded the places where they had worked overseas. Dr Watson, introduced at the start of *A Study in Scarlet*, could well have passed as one of the many veterans in Conan Doyle's circle in this south coast resort. He may have spent time living there because in 'The Adventure of the Resident Patient' he finds himself in London on a close, rainy day yearning for the shingle of Southsea and the glades of the nearby New Forest. (It has inconclusively been suggested that Conan Doyle drew on a Southsea doctor called James Watson for the name of his detective's companion.) Before meeting Holmes, Watson had served in the British army in Afghanistan in a campaign aimed largely to protect the territorial integrity of India, the jewel in the Imperial crown. He had been

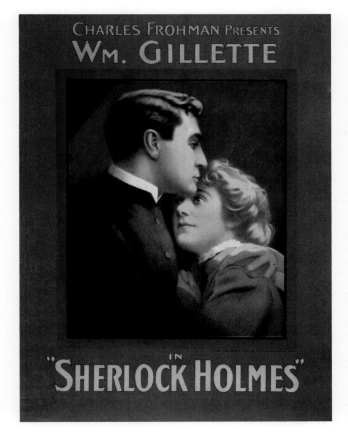

wounded at the Battle of Maiwand in 1880 and returned to London to pick up the threads of his medical career.

Dr Watson was the first of many characters in the Sherlock Holmes stories who travel from distant outposts of the Empire to make their mark on and, sometimes, haunt Britain. *A Study in Scarlet* appeared only months before Conan Doyle published an intriguing non-Sherlockian novella, *The Mystery of Cloomber*; this story involves three Brahmin priests, who travelled from India to Scotland to avenge the death of an elderly priest in a massacre in the Hindu Kush in the First Afghan War (1838–42). Having used psychic means to terrify the British general who authorized this massacre, they pursued him to Scotland and killed him. However, Conan Doyle showed his limited understanding of India by giving non-Hindu names to two of the Brahmin priests. His approach reflects an earlier stage of Britain's engagement with its colonies, when British scholars made well-meaning efforts to understand the cultures of the people they were ruling. The father of the story's narrator, John Fothergill West, is an Orientalist scholar who, after a career as a solicitor, retired into genteel poverty, 'consol[ed] … with the aphorisms and precepts of Firdousi, Omar Khayyam, and others of his Eastern favourites'.

As *The Mystery of Cloomber* suggested, Britain's relationship with her colonies had become more involved by the late 1880s. Those colonies now sent the 'mother country' foodstuffs, such as wheat, tea and sugar, and raw materials, including cotton, jute and spices, all of which affected the lifestyles of the British people and made some rich. And then there were the more intangible consequences, which ranged from the expertise accumulated by professionals such as Dr Watson, through the silk products, tapestries and other artefacts acquired by individuals in distant climes, to the more personal, emotional attachments, including the grudges which led to the murder in this story of a top-ranking soldier who held the Victoria Cross. All this was amplified after European countries began the scramble for Africa in earnest during this decade, and empire was no longer a dirty word.

In *The Sign of Four*, his second outing following *A Study in Scarlet*, Sherlock Holmes was required to solve a mystery with a particularly colonial core – a murder involving the attempt by a former British convict, Jonathan Small, to recover a fortune he had shared with a prison guard in the notorious Indian penal colony, the Andaman Islands. In this quest, Small employs a pygmy Andaman islander called Tonga, who is skilled at killing people with poisoned darts blown from a pipe. The text refers frequently to this colonial background, moving from Agra at the time of the Indian Mutiny to the penal colony on the Andaman Islands. When Holmes and Watson visit the South London house of Thaddeus Sholto (one of the sons of the prison guard), they are let in by a *khitmatgar*, or servant, in traditional Indian garb of yellow turban, white, loose-fitting clothes and a yellow sash. The place is decked out as if from an Orientalist dream:

> The richest and glossiest of curtains and tapestries draped the walls, looped back here and there to expose some richly mounted painting or Oriental vase. The carpet was of amber and black, so soft and so thick that the foot sank pleasantly into it, as into a bed of moss. Two great tiger skins thrown athwart it increased the suggestion of Eastern luxury, as did a huge hookah which stood upon a mat in the corner. A lamp in the fashion of a silver dove was hung from an almost invisible golden wire in the centre of the room. As it burned it filled the air with a subtle and aromatic odour.

Tonga, the tiny Andaman islander, is presented in less benevolent terms. He is a 'little hell-hound' and his people are:

> … naturally hideous, having large, misshapen heads, small fierce eyes, and distorted features. Their feet and hands, however, are remarkably small. So intractable and fierce are they, that all the efforts of the British officials have failed to win them over in any degree. They have always been a terror to shipwrecked crews, braining the survivors with their stone-headed clubs or shooting them with their poisoned arrows. These massacres are invariably concluded by a cannibal feast.

Such descriptions point to the sense of cultural supremacism and racism which had become widespread at the time, and which was implicit in the ideology of imperialism. This was carried into the thinking about an Anglo-Saxon federation. As Conan Doyle himself once said, this alliance was 'rooted in a shared language and strengthened by various phases of genetic mingling' which

Opposite John Watson was wounded at the Battle of Maiwand during the Second Anglo-Afghan War, on 27 July 1880.

Left First book edition of The Mystery of Cloomber, *published in 1888 by Ward & Downey.*

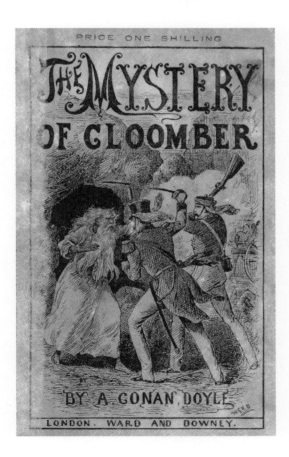

PRICE ONE SHILLING

THE MYSTERY OF CLOOMBER

BY A. CONAN DOYLE

LONDON. WARD AND DOWNEY.

Above Engraving of Ballarat from a gold mine on Black Hill, Victoria, Australia (c.1880).

he regarded as unambiguously benign – evidence, perhaps, of 'a great hand blending the seeds.'

Like those crossing the Atlantic, ex-colonials often returned home seeking peace and respectability in England. As well as Sholto, a classic example is John Wilson, whom Holmes identifies as the killer of Charles McCarthy in 'The Boscombe Valley Mystery'. Wilson lives in the Herefordshire countryside with a close group of men who have made money in Australia. The story states specifically that 'they appear to have avoided the society of the neighbouring English families and to have led retired lives.' With great ingenuity, Holmes unravels that what they have in common is their membership of the Ballarat Gang, which – back in the 1860s – had robbed a gold convoy making its way to Melbourne. Another with a similar backstory is James Armitage in 'The Adventure of the Gloria Scott' who, having been convicted and transported to Australia for embezzlement, escapes in dramatic fashion and makes his fortune in the Antipodes. He then returns to England, where he adopts the surname Trevor and lives impeccably as a justice of the peace in rural Norfolk, where he fathers Holmes's college friend, Victor Trevor.

Often the returnee is a former soldier, such as Colonel Barclay, an officer in the celebrated Irish regiment the Royal Munsters; in 'The Adventure of the Crooked Man' Barclay comes back to live close to the barracks in Aldershot. In 'The Adventure of the Blanched Soldier' the Boer War veteran James Dodd consults Holmes about the disappearance of his friend Godfrey Emsworth with whom he had served in the Middlesex Corps. Emsworth is holed up in Tuxbury Old Park in Bedfordshire – the family home of his father Colonel Emsworth, a Crimean War V.C. – where he appears to have brought back a malignant memento of the colonies: a bad case of leprosy. An omniscient doctor, of the type often consulted by Holmes, diagnoses his condition as ichthyosis, a scaly pseudo-leprosy that can in fact be cured.

In 'The Adventure of the Devil's Foot', Dr Leon Sterndale, displays a distinctive skill set and carries back a different souvenir from his time overseas. He's 'the great lion-hunter and explorer' who kills the vile Mortimer Tregennis with a rare poison known as Devil's Foot Root, which is used as an ordeal poison by medicine men 'in the Ubanghi country' in the modern Republic of the Congo. Taking justice into his own hands again, Holmes sees this murder as a crime of passion and allows Sterndale back to Central Africa to carry on his work.

The final strand in Holmes's engagement with the outside world is evident in his approach to Europe. He's clearly a European at heart – conversant with the works of Goethe and the lesser-known German Romantic writer Jean Paul, familiar with the operas of Meyerbeer and Wagner, and at home in a number of European capitals. As the King of Bohemia tells him at the start of 'A Scandal in Bohemia', ' Your recent services to one of the royal houses of Europe have shown that you are one who may safely be trusted with matters which are of an importance which can hardly be exaggerated.'

Railways had, by then, opened up the Continent for travel – not just for pleasure, but also for criminal activity. In *A Study in Scarlet*, Jefferson Hope tracks Drebber and Stangerson, the Mormons he blames for his wife's death, through Europe:

> When he reached St Petersburg, they had departed for Paris; and when he followed them there, he learned that they had just set off for Copenhagen. At the Danish capital he was again a few days late, for they had journeyed on to London, where he at last succeeded in running them to earth.

And where criminals venture, Holmes is never far behind. When Baron Gruner is mentioned in 'The Adventure of the Illustrious Client', Holmes quickly identifies him as the 'Austrian murderer', and, on being questioned why he had jumped to that conclusion, declares:

> It is my business to follow the details of Continental crime. Who could possibly have read what happened at Prague and have any doubts as to the man's guilt! It was a purely technical legal point and the suspicious death of a witness that saved him! I am as sure that he killed his wife when the so-called 'accident' happened in the Splugen Pass as if I had seen him do it.

Europe is also at the centre of important diplomatic activity. The subject matter of 'The Adventure of the Naval Treaty' (first published in 1893) proved highly topical, as it came just as France and Russia were signing a secret treaty to guard them against Germany and her allies, Austria-Hungary and Italy, who joined together to form the Triple Alliance. In the story, Holmes is called upon

Left 'He tore the mask from his face', an 1891 illustration by Sidney Paget for 'A Scandal in Bohemia'.

to help Watson's old school friend, Percy Phelps, who has run into deep trouble in his high-flying job in the civil service because he has lost the text of a vital naval treaty between Britain and Italy, after being entrusted to copy it by his uncle, the foreign minister. In reassuring Phelps that Holmes is the man to assist him Watson says, 'To my certain knowledge he has acted on behalf of three of the reigning houses of Europe in very vital matters.'

A decade or so later, Britain's relationship with Europe had become more complicated, as she began to fret about German expansionism. The dating of 'The Adventure of the Second Stain' (first published in 1904) is equivocal. By the time Watson committed the story to paper, Holmes had already retired to the Sussex countryside to take up beekeeping and the events in it are said to have happened in 'a year, and even in a decade, that shall be nameless'. This is generally considered to have been 1888. As noted above, it tells how Lord Bellinger, the Prime Minister (usually equated with Lord Salisbury), visits Holmes to enlist his help in finding a vital letter which has disappeared from the safe of his anachronistically named Minister for European Affairs. It is clear that this involves a vital matter of the state. In answer to a question, Bellinger explains to the detective:

You take me into regions of high international politics. But if you consider the European situation you will have no difficulty in perceiving the motive. The whole of Europe is an armed camp. There is a double league which makes a fair balance of military power. Great Britain holds the scales. If Britain were driven into war with one confederacy, it would assure the supremacy of the other confederacy, whether they joined in the war or not. Do you follow?

To which Holmes replies, 'Very clearly.'

Holmes was simply reflecting developments in international relations as Britain began to understand that the main threat to her shores and to her Empire was from Europe. This ramped up from 1897 when Germany began to expand its naval fleet. Britain responded in 1906 by launching HMS *Dreadnought*, the first of a new class of powerful battleships driven by steam turbine. This led to a protracted naval arms race which, although reined back around 1912 for reasons of expense, nevertheless stoked up the rivalry which led to the First World War two years later.

Right Relief sculpture celebrating the Triple Alliance of 1882 between Germany, Austria-Hungary and Italy.

Opposite 'A nobleman', an 1893 illustration by Sidney Paget for 'The Adventure of the Naval Treaty'.

"A NOBLEMAN."

As a fervent nationalist as well as imperialist, Conan Doyle supported every effort to build up Britain's military and naval strength in the face of German threats. He lobbied for rearmament and for a Channel Tunnel which he argued would be of vital importance in the event of a naval blockade of Britain. 'What would be the condition of our food supplies if there were 25 hostile submarines off the Kent coast and 25 in the Irish Channel?' he recalled in his autobiography *Memories and Adventures*.

In September 1914, as Britain entered the First World War, Conan Doyle published *To Arms!*, a pamphlet designed to encourage domestic recruitment and to explain Britain's war aims to sometimes sceptical countries overseas. Just before that, in August, as revealed in the story *His Last Bow* (itself published in September 1917), Holmes emerged from retirement to foil an attempt by the German agent von Bork to steal a critical document relating to naval signals. According to Dr Watson's epigraph to the eponymous book in which this story is collected, 'The approach of the German war caused [Holmes], however, to lay his remarkable combination of intellectual and practical activity at the disposal of the government, with historical results which are recounted in 'His Last Bow'.' The great

detective had been visited in Sussex by both the Prime Minister and the Foreign Minister, and it was time for him, like his creator, to put aside beekeeping and return to the sort of challenge and involvement in the outside world that he loved best.

Below 'Dreadnought' and 'Victory' at Portsmouth, *oil on canvas, by Henry J. Morgan (1839–1917).*

THE ADVANCE
OF SCIENCE

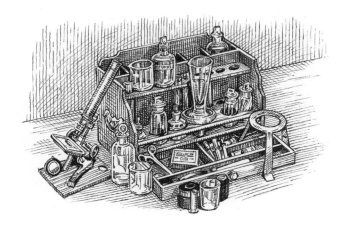

It's a coincidence that Arthur Conan Doyle's birth in May 1859 was followed six months later by one of the defining moments in the history of science – the publication of Charles Darwin's epoch-defining book *On the Origin of Species*. It means the author of Sherlock Holmes grew up in a world where the accepted cultural framework had recently changed, and rather radically. The world was no longer defined by God; man and his intellectual curiosity had wrested control.

Using the data he had meticulously collected over the years, Darwin pulled together all the ideas about natural selection that had been floating around the scientific community and gave them intellectual respectability. Thereafter, the theory that humans had evolved from a series of random mutations became accepted. Man was now officially descended from apes rather than angels. And if traditional religion had suffered a critical blow to its credibility, science now cemented its position as the accepted way to look at and to understand the physical world. Conan Doyle's life would be different, along with that of his brilliant fictional detective.

Of course, science didn't just appear in 1859, and that just happened to be the year of the birth of Arthur Conan

Doyle. (Sherlock Holmes was only a few years older, having been born, according to the accepted evidence in his stories, on 6 January 1854, and therefore his life was very much played out in the modern scientific era.) The practice of science had been developing, from its origins in Egypt and Mesopotamia four millennia earlier, through a golden age among the classical Greeks. It had been nurtured by the Arabs in the Middle Ages, and brought into practical use in Western Europe in the seventeenth and eighteenth centuries, when advances in mathematics, astronomy, mechanics and chemistry helped spawn the Industrial Revolution. Underpinned by the insights of Enlightenment philosophers, who stressed scepticism, rationality and empiricism, the spirit of scientific experimentation and enquiry had thoroughly permeated British society by the Victorian era. This was the spirit which inspired Sherlock Holmes.

In the process, science had been professionalized. It had developed from a branch of metaphysics, often known as natural philosophy, into a system of experimentally based knowledge. Sherlock Holmes must have been teasing Dr Watson when, at the start of *A Study in Scarlet*, he expressed no awareness of the Scots-born polymath Thomas Carlyle. He later backtracked in *The Sign of Four*, but rather

Above *'I've found it! I've found it!'*
an 1893 illustration by George
Hutchinson (1852–1942) for
A Study in Scarlet.

Opposite above *'Not a brawler', a*
caricature of Samuel Wilberforce,
Bishop of Oxford, published in
Vanity Fair *in 1869.*

Opposite below *Title page of the*
1906 edition of Charles Darwin's
The Origin of Species.

demeaned Carlyle by claiming to see him as a follower of the German Romantic philosopher Johann Paul Richter (known as Jean Paul, in honour of his mentor Rousseau). Nevertheless, it was Carlyle who, as early as 1829, grasped the intellectual trends when he wrote in the *Edinburgh Review* that 'the Metaphysical and Moral Sciences are falling into decay, while the Physical are engrossing every day more respect and attention', because 'what cannot be investigated and understood mechanically cannot be investigated and understood at all.' It was this mechanically or experimentally based system of knowledge which was celebrated shortly before Holmes's birth in the Great Exhibition of 1851.

This gathering of the best in early Victorian industry and manufacturing in – to give it its full title – The Great Exhibition of the Works of Industry of All Nations – was a testament to science's contribution to the modern world, taking in fields such as engineering, geology, metallurgy, chemistry and electricity. Its patron was Prince Albert, the Prince Consort, later President of the British Association for the Advancement of Science (BAAS), where his inaugural address in 1859 noted, 'The man of Science observes what he intends to observe, and knows why he intends it.' This was modus operandi was close to Holmes's, as revealed in his comment to Inspector Lestrade in 'The Adventure of Silver Blaze' where, when the lumbering police detective confesses he cannot imagine how he had failed to find the remnants of a match at the crime scene, Holmes replied, 'It was invisible, buried in the mud. I only saw it because I was looking for it.' It was at the BAAS annual meeting in Oxford the following year (1860) that, in a discussion of the recent publication of *On the Origin of Species*, the Anglican Bishop Samuel Wilberforce, asked 'Darwin's bulldog' Thomas Huxley if he claimed descent from an ape through his grandfather or grandmother, and Huxley replied he didn't mind, but would be ashamed to be associated with someone who used his great gifts to obscure the truth.

Less than thirty years later, in his novel *A Study in Scarlet*, Conan Doyle would introduce Sherlock Holmes pootling about in a chemical laboratory at St Bartholomew's Hospital in London. He's conducting an experiment which he claims will lead to 'the most practical medico-legal discovery for years'. And he seems to have all the trappings of a proper scientist, albeit maybe of the amateur variety. He's in a 'lofty chamber, lined and littered with countless bottles. Broad, low tables were scattered about, which bristled with retorts, test tubes and little Bunsen lamps with their blue flickering flames.' He's enthusing about a new test which can detect the history of stains, usually on clothes. Previously detectives had had to rely on the old guaiacum test, which Holmes describes as 'very clumsy and uncertain'. 'But now', he professes, 'we have the Sherlock Holmes test', and there will no longer be any problems about identifying whether the stains come from blood, mud or rust.'

It's the approach of a dedicated researcher, one who likes to do his own experiments and develop his own techniques in keeping with the latest scientific techniques of his day. But when Watson gets to know Holmes (and lives with him in Baker Street), the latter's loftier scientific credentials become hazier. In Watson's list of his new friend's academic abilities (also in *A Study in Scarlet*), the only field in which the detective shows real aptitude is chemistry, where his knowledge is rated as 'profound'. But his understanding of other areas of science is less note-worthy; his botany is 'Variable. Well up in belladonna, opium, and poisons generally. Knows nothing of practical gardening.' While his geology is 'practical, but limited'. Even his command of anatomy is only graded as 'accurate, but unsystematic'. And as for astronomy, which Conan Doyle certainly considered important, Holmes's grasp of the subject is assessed as 'nil'.

He is evidently something of a maverick in his field. This is how he is first presented to Watson by a mutual friend called Stamford who had been the doctor's dresser at Bart's: Stamford describes Holmes as 'a little queer in his ideas – an enthusiast in some branches of science.' When Watson asks if Holmes is a medical student, Stamford says no. The former dresser admits that Holmes is 'well up in anatomy' and is 'a first-class chemist', but 'his studies are very desultory and eccentric', even if 'he has amassed a lot of out-of-the-way knowledge which would astonish his professors.' The picture does indeed emerge of someone who has studied widely, if haphazardly. This is corroborated when Watson takes further stock of Holmes:

Neither did he appear to have pursued any course of reading which might fit him for a degree in science or any other recognized portal which would give him an entrance into the learned world. Yet his zeal for certain studies was remarkable, and within eccentric limits his knowledge was so extraordinarily ample and minute that his observations have fairly astounded me.

It's all a bit confusing, but it is such ambivalences that help make Holmes such an enduring character. The evidence suggests he has been to university (that reference to him 'astonish[ing] his professors'), yet he hasn't done the necessary study to fit him for a degree in science. Only in a later story, 'The Adventure of the Musgrave Ritual', is it confirmed (by Holmes himself) that he had indeed been to university:

When I first came up to London I had rooms in Montague Street, just round the corner from the British Museum, and there I waited, filling in my too abundant leisure time by studying all those branches of science which might make me more efficient. Now and again cases came in my way, principally through the introduction of old fellow-students, for during my last years at the university there was a good deal of talk there about myself and my methods.

There is considerable debate among Sherlockian enthusiasts as to whether his alma mater was Oxford or Cambridge. But wherever he studied, his modus operandi was not traditionally academic.

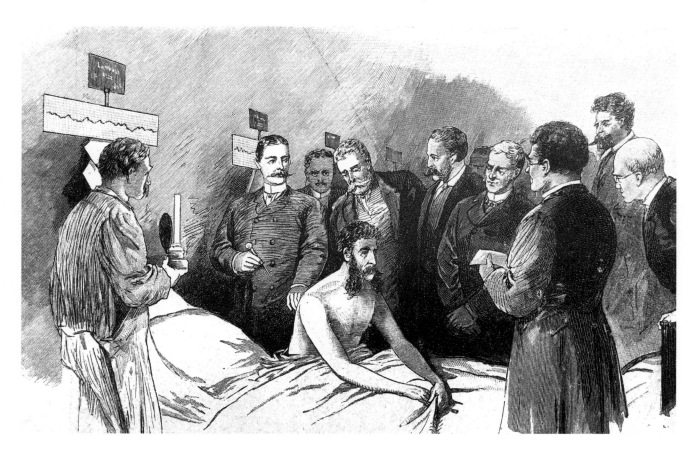

Watson's personal view of his new companion's intellectual credentials is hardly enhanced early in his tenancy in Baker Street when, while waiting for Holmes to finish his breakfast, he chances upon a magazine article titled 'The Book of Life'. This addresses aspects of both philosophy and science in its assertion that 'from a drop of water … a logician could infer the possibility of an Atlantic or a Niagara without having seen or heard of one or the other. So all life is a great chain, the nature of which is known whenever we are shown a single link of it.' Leading to conclusions which he describes 'as infallible as so many propositions of Euclid', the writer also suggests that it is possible 'by a momentary expression, a twitch of a muscle or a glance of an eye, to fathom a man's inmost thoughts.' Watson spontaneously voices his disapproval, declaring that such ideas are impractical, whereupon Holmes reveals not only that he himself wrote the article but also that its conclusions are eminently practical as he himself depends on them for his livelihood as the world's only 'consulting detective'.

Sherlock Holmes was here clearly demonstrating his appreciation of conventional science. His comment about being able to infer a great ocean from a drop of water harks back to the French naturalist and geologist Georges Cuvier. He picks this up in a subsequent short story 'The Five Orange Pips', where he compares his own professional approach to that of Cuvier: 'As Cuvier could correctly describe a whole animal by the contemplation of a single bone, so the observer who has thoroughly understood one link in a series of incidents should be able to accurately state all the other ones, both before and after.'

Cuvier, the so-called 'founding father of paleontology', is the only established scientist mentioned by name by Holmes, even if he's hardly modern by the time Conan Doyle is writing. The detective doesn't refer to any of the later nineteenth century giants of science, such as the British surgeon Joseph Lister or the German microbiologist Robert Koch. Even Darwin has no more than an oblique reference in the canon. On one occasion Watson recalls an exchange where his friend asks:

'Do you remember what Darwin says about music? He claims that the power of producing and appreciating it existed among the human race long before the power of speech was arrived at. Perhaps that is why we are so subtly influenced by it. There are vague memories in our souls of those

Opposite Microbiologist Robert Koch (1843–1910) demonstrates a vaccination to a group of doctors.

Above Baron Georges Cuvier (1769–1832) Reunites the Documents for his Work on Fossil Bones, *fresco by Theobald Chartran (1849–1907).*

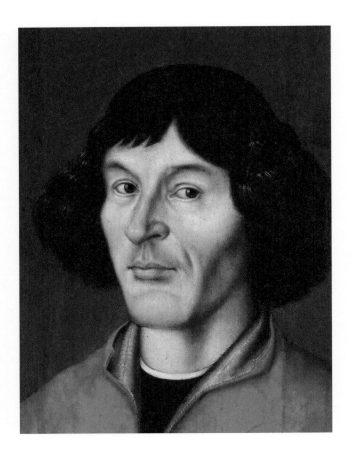

Above Portrait of Nicolaus Copernicus (c.1580), whose heliocentric model was seemingly irrelevant to Holmes's understanding of the heavens.

Opposite left 'Finally he examined with his glass the word upon the wall' a 1904 illustration by Frederic Dorr Steele (1873–1944) for A Study in Scarlet.

Opposite right The cover illustration for this 1954 edition of The Sign of Four *shows Holmes demonstrating his skills of abduction.*

misty centuries when the world was in its childhood.' 'That's a rather broad idea,' I remarked. 'One's ideas must be as broad as Nature if they are to interpret Nature,' he answered.

This statement only emphasizes Holmes's idiosyncratic approach to the accumulation of knowledge. This conversation began with him showing ignorance of the Copernican Revolution, the discovery that the earth revolves around the sun, which is at the heart of the modern world view. (In this way he reinforces Watson's observation about his lack of knowledge of astronomy.) But Holmes remained nonplussed. He said that it didn't matter to him whether the earth went round the sun or the moon (or indeed what exactly Thomas Carlyle wrote or said). He simply didn't want to lumber his brain with too much detail. He regarded it as an empty attic where he could store items for later use, but he shouldn't let it get too crowded.

Instead, Holmes's business (which early on is revealed as a 'consulting detective') is shown to rely on the basic technique of observing and making deductions from what he sees. In this scientifically approved manner, he had, as Stamford stated, amassed (and presumably, according to his own comments, discarded at the appropriate time) a lot of out-of-the-way knowledge, particularly when it relates to his own field of criminology and forensics (a subset of science which will be dealt with separately in the next chapter). Among his accomplishments is a series of monographs which, according to Watson in *The Sign of Four*, he has 'been guilty of'. One is called 'Upon the Distinction between the Ashes of the Various Tobaccos' in which he analyzes the ash made by 140 different types of tobacco substance. Another itemizes the influence of trades on the hands of individuals, showing the differences to be found in the hands of slaters, sailors, cork-cutters, compositors and weavers. But although these works take a scientific approach, they are really tools to aid his profession as a consulting detective.

Conan Doyle evidently regarded Holmes's method as scientific, because, unusually, he gave the title 'The Science of Deduction' to separate chapters in both of his first two books, *A Study in Scarlet* and *The Sign of Four*. Commentators have argued that Holmes's method was not really deduction (meaning the reaching of a conclusion from generally established statements or facts) or even induction (the inferring of what might have happened from a series of statements or facts), but abduction (meaning the formation of possible hypotheses about what might have occurred and then concluding on the best balance of probabilities as to what actually happened).

This is indeed the creative detective's (or scientist's) modus operandi. Interestingly, around the time of Sherlock Holmes's inception, the concept of abduction was being given a new lease of academic life in the United States by the mathematician and philosopher Charles S. Peirce. Conan Doyle is likely to have heard about him in the context of some of his favourite American thinkers, such as Ralph Waldo Emerson and Oliver Wendell Holmes. For his work in this and related fields, Pierce is often described as the founder of semiotics – the study of signs in a social context. As the Italian critic Umberto Eco has pointed out, this was precisely Holmes's method.

Holmes does seem to meet the UK Science Council's modern definition of the job of a scientist as 'someone who systematically gathers and uses research and evidence, to make hypotheses and test them, to gain and share understanding and knowledge'. Holmes himself indicates that his calling is scientific when he pronounces, 'Detection is, or ought to be, an exact science, and should be treated in the same cold and unemotional manner'. And he is happy to be described as hardly human – an 'automaton' who has put aside the 'softer passions' and become 'the most perfect reasoning and observing machine that the world has seen'.

For all that, and as further indication of his contrariness, Holmes does not pay much attention to other scientists in his exploits. It has been noted how little he acknowledges his historical predecessors in this field. And scientists in general play little part in his work as a consulting detective. According to Marshall S. Berdan in his essay in 'My Scientific Methods', as many as sixty men of science appear in the canon (but no women), although the word 'scientist' is only used five times. Scientists crop up in Holmes's work, but remain peripheral to it. They are friends or acquaintances, often medical doctors, sometimes engineers (as in 'The Adventure of the Engineer's Thumb'). They seldom offer their professional scientific expertise in any sort of criminal investigation. That does not detract from his being a scientific detective. But he is only really interested in science where it affects his profession as a detective. Thus, he is an early practitioner of the science of forensics – technically, the application of science to legal problems.

Conan Doyle's own development as a scientist is easier to chart. He had little experience of science, with its specific ideas and techniques, until 1876, when at the age of

seventeen, he went to university in Edinburgh, the city of his birth, to study medicine. Coming from a family of artists, the practice of observing his environment and taking note was instilled in him from an early age. But at Stonyhurst College, the Jesuit public school he attended in Lancashire, he was poor at science. When he sat his mock matriculation exams, he admitted to his mother that his worst performing paper was chemistry (which turned out to be Holmes's trump suit). When he had to sit an additional exam in pursuit of a bursary to finance his university studies, it emerged that he had never learned trigonometry or conic sections, or dipped into books five and six of Euclid, references to all of which were later found in the Sherlock Holmes stories.

Studying medicine at university changed all that. It gave Conan Doyle not only a profession, but a particular way of looking at the world. Talking to students at St Mary's Hospital, London, in 1910, he waxed lyrical about how a medical training helped induce a 'healthy scepticism', as well as 'the desire to prove every fact, and only to reason from such proved facts – these are the foundations for all thought'. This ingrained inquisitiveness produced a scientific turn of mind; it was the foundation of his career, and that of his creation Sherlock Holmes.

He was helped by the fact that Edinburgh had been the birthplace of the Scottish Enlightenment, where thinkers such as David Hume had honed the ideas of empiricism, the philosophical tradition at the heart of modern science, and one much revered in the university medical school. There, Conan Doyle followed in the steps of pioneers such as James Young Simpson, who discovered chloroform, and Joseph Lister, who introduced antiseptics into surgery. Conan Doyle lapped up their pragmatic enquiring approach. He wasn't particularly interested in any grand theory of science at this stage. He was more intent on observing the techniques of his own teachers – contemporary giants of his profession such as Professor Robert Christison and Professor Thomas Richard Fraser, who had shifted the medical department's emphasis from anatomy to pharmacology. This helped inculcate in the young Conan Doyle a passion for the meticulous investigation of any medicine he came across, even if that meant personally ingesting potentially harmful alkaloids – all in the interest of scientific experimentation. In this way he acquired the precise knowledge of drugs and poisons he was later to put to literary use in Sherlock Holmes stories like 'The Adventure of the Sussex Vampire'.

His most influential teacher was Dr Joseph Bell, the Professor of Surgery who also did the rounds in the Royal Infirmary where he adopted the student Conan Doyle as his outpatient clerk. Bell was famous for his meticulous observation of his patients, not simply looking for medical symptoms but for all sorts of personal traits. According to Conan Doyle's autobiography *Memories and Adventures*, Bell could tell from a man's appearance and behaviour that, for example, he had recently served in a Highland regiment in Barbados. He worked on clues such as the man's failure to remove his hat, which marked him out as a soldier, and his condition of elephantiasis, which, according to Bell, showed he had been in the West Indies. It was a short step from this to Sherlock Holmes's assertion that Dr Watson had been in Afghanistan at the start of *A Study in Scarlet*, and his reasons for it. The whole Holmesian technique of investigation was based on such principles.

It wasn't just aids to detection which flourished in Edinburgh. In 1866, when Conan Doyle was a young boy, a permanent underwater telegraph cable was laid between Britain and the United States. There had been one a few years earlier, which had enabled Queen Victoria to communicate briefly with US President James Buchanan. But transmission speeds were painfully slow, and the project was abandoned after three weeks. A second cable was laid in 1865, but it broke. The third, laid the following year by SS *Great Eastern* (the largest steamship in the world at the time, designed by Isambard Kingdom Brunel), was as much a symbol of the expanding, questing, scientifically literate, industrialized world as anything. Over the next two decades underwater telegraph cables linked all corners of the globe (or initially, at least, the British Empire) and proved vital for communications.

Between 1872 and 1876 (the year Conan Doyle first enrolled at the University of Edinburgh) the ground-breaking *Challenger* expedition charted the depths and the composition of the world's oceans. This expedition, which established the science of oceanography on the same level as astronomy, was coordinated – at least scientifically – from Edinburgh, where Sir Charles Wyville Thomson held the chair of natural history. In his autobiography *Memories and Adventures* Conan Doyle writes about being taught by Wyville Thomson, whom he describes more specifically as a zoologist, 'fresh from his *Challenger* expedition'. He later named his fictional scientist explorer in *The Lost World* Professor Challenger, who was based partly on Wyville Thomson and partly on another of his non-medical

Opposite The entrance courtyard of Old College, University of Edinburgh, c.1880.

Above Portrait of Joseph Bell, Conan Doyle's tutor at Edinburgh.

Above Conan Doyle in 1882 outside Bush Villas in Southsea in Hampshire, where he worked as a GP after graduating.

Opposite Conan Doyle dressed as Professor Challenger, who first appeared in his novel The Lost World *(1912).*

teachers, William Rutherford, professor of physiology – a squat figure with wild 'Assyrian' hair and a booming voice. He called these teachers 'remarkable men', even if, in his estimation, the most notable among them was Joseph Bell.

After graduating, Conan Doyle took a job as a GP in Southsea, a suburb of Portsmouth. He juggled his professional practice with his efforts to develop a career as a writer, sending stories to publications such as *Blackwood's Magazine* or *The Cornhill Magazine*. In his day-to-day life, dealing with his patients, he strove to give the impression of a level-headed doctor imbued with a solid sense of practical science. He joined the respectable Portsmouth Literary and Scientific Society. In his occasional journalism, he contributed a piece to *Good Words* on bacteriology which paid homage to solid investigative pioneers in that field such as Louis Pasteur and Robert Koch, and he strongly advocated the practice of vaccination. He wrote to the *Daily Telegraph* arguing that, for public health reasons, prostitutes should be rounded up and inspected for sexual diseases. And, as a keen amateur photographer who sent articles to the *British Journal of Photography*, he was careful to distance himself from a contemporary idea that it was possible to photograph spirit forms.

While at university he turned his back on the Catholicism of his birth and, to the horror of his family, pronounced himself an agnostic. Like many young men, he had begun to reflect the questioning spirit of the age which followed the publication of Charles Darwin's *On the Origin of Species*. As he himself put it in *Memories and Adventures*:

> These were the years when [T.H.] Huxley, [John] Tyndall, [Charles] Darwin, Herbert Spencer and John Stuart Mill were our chief philosophers, and that even the man in the street felt the strong sweeping current of their thought, while to the young student, eager and impressionable, it was overwhelming.

So, on top of his empirical education in Edinburgh, Conan Doyle came to maturity during that post-Darwin period when the climate of intellectual opinion was changing. People were looking at the world with a fresh, critical perspective, casting aside long-held religious-inspired certainties and coming up with new ideas about mankind's place in the world, which incorporated disciplines like cosmology, geology, biology, psychology, paleontology and even history. Underlying all this was the need, so often mentioned by Sherlock Holmes, to observe and take note.

It soon became clear that, however much Conan Doyle welcomed this sort of enquiry, he himself was never happy about its full implications. Perhaps it was his Catholic upbringing, but he always felt there was another dimension to consciousness, one beyond the scope and understanding of objective science, perhaps more akin to the religious idea of the soul, which was present in life and which, he later strongly advocated, could survive death.

So began his life-long personal battle between the opposing claims of science and religion. It was a conflict which manifested itself in several clear dichotomies in his own life and work, even stretching to the differences in mentality between the supposedly rational detective Sherlock Holmes and his more 'romantic' companion Dr John Watson.

He explored this in a book called *The Narrative of John Smith*, which centred on the struggles of the eponymous doctor to square his belief in progress (again promoting the work of scientists such as Pasteur) with his interest in matters of the spirit. One influence he acknowledged in this book (written in 1884 at the start of his career as a GP in Southsea) was a traveller and intellectual called Winwood Reade (nephew of the novelist Charles Reade, author of one of his favourite novels *The Cloister and the Hearth*). Conan Doyle referred to *The Martyrdom of Man*, Winwood Reade's panoramic history of the human race, as 'one of the most remarkable (books) ever penned'. And the reason was that Reade was a vociferous advocate of the sort of Darwin-inspired agnosticism that profoundly influenced Conan Doyle's thinking at the time. In *The Martyrdom of Man* Reade went as far as to state that 'Christianity is not in accordance with the cultivated mind. ... It is ... a superstition; and ought to be destroyed.'

But Conan Doyle also had his doubts about Reade's approach, adopting a compromise position which commentators have likened to the North American philosophical tradition of transcendentalism, often identified with Ralph Waldo Emerson, but also manifest in the writings of another US thinker and medical reformer, Oliver Wendell Holmes; whose book of essays *The Autocrat of the Breakfast-Table* (1858) and its successors Conan Doyle loved, and whose name he adopted for his soon-to-be-realized fictional detective.

Above Illustration of a séance, showing a floating guitar and a ghostly hand (c.1887).

Opposite An 1891 engraving showing Robert Koch in his laboratory.

Although he wrote *The Narrative of John Smith* as a young man, Conan Doyle appears to have become embarrassed by its contents, because he subsequently claimed to have lost it, and the manuscript was not rediscovered and published until the early twenty-first century. But that did not stop him maintaining a quiet interest in questions about the conflicting claims of the mind and spirit which he justified by investing them with scientific credentials. This tallied with the widespread post-Darwinian fascination with psychic and extra-sensory phenomena, including levitation, seances and mesmerism. A body of distinguished scientists even formed the Society for Psychical Research in 1882 to pursue this area of study. Conan Doyle followed these developments closely, carried out his own seances, and wrote for a magazine called *Light* which reported on this subject.

All the time, he successfully pursued his callings as a doctor and as an author, another of the great balancing acts in his life. But it was becoming increasingly clear that he was hedging his bets in his approach to the outside world: was it to be based on his Edinburgh-inspired scientific empiricism or was he to incorporate this with his sense that there was another dimension to reality and existence?

His career took a turn in 1890 when he decided to quit his job as a GP and to seek fame and fortune as a specialist in London (while all the time maintaining his interest in writing). The way this came about is informative. He had clearly been thinking about a move from the south coast. But the specific stimulus was his curiosity about the work of the German physician Robert Koch, who was widely regarded as the father of microbiology.

Over the previous couple of decades Koch had made major advances in verifying the germ theory of disease – in particular, by confirming (though other scientists were also involved) that anthrax, cholera and, in particular, tuberculosis were infections caused by bacteria. It was a period of exciting developments in the theory and prevention of disease, with both Koch and the Frenchman Louis Pasteur leading the way with new discoveries, while building up a fierce rivalry in the process. Conan Doyle's interest in this field was further sparked when he learned that Koch had claimed to have discovered a cure for tuberculosis and a colleague of his was intending to give a demonstration of this in Berlin. (Conan Doyle had a personal involvement in that his wife Louise was soon to be diagnosed with that disease – which led to her death in

1906 – and it is likely that he, as a doctor, had intimations of this prognosis.)

As he explained in *Memories and Adventures*, Conan Doyle immediately had an 'irresistible impulse' to go to Berlin to witness what he realized would be a historical event. Neatly combining his twin careers, he prevailed on W.T. Stead, editor of the *Review of Reviews*, to let him report on this. (This was at a time when popular magazines for all the family were beginning to make a mark on the publishing world. They often featured educational topics, particularly science. Another was *The Strand Magazine*, where Conan Doyle's short stories would famously soon feature.)

Conan Doyle's trip to Berlin was not entirely successful. Koch's colleague was reluctant to let him witness his presentation – an indication of the international competitiveness then prevalent in the field of medical research. Koch's spat with Pasteur was an example, reflecting German-French antagonism, which had only recently surfaced in the Franco-Prussian war, and pointing to increasingly nationalistic and often imperialistic rivalries.

Apart from reinforcing his interest in disease transmission (a theme taken up in Sherlock Holmes stories, such as 'The Adventure of the Dying Detective'), Conan

Doyle's trip to Berlin was useful because it led to his meeting Malcolm Morris, a Harley Street specialist, who suggested his medical talents were wasted in the provinces and urged him to develop his professional interest in eyes as a consultant ophthalmologist in London. To do that he would need to spend a short time studying in Vienna, the accepted centre for research into the eye. This he duly did, at the start of 1891, before returning to London to follow up this new (for him) specialism in Wimpole Street.

But his medical practice did not fare well. And by then he was occupied with other matters. He had acquired a literary agent, A.P. Watt, who began sending his short stories featuring the detective Sherlock Holmes to *The Strand Magazine*. These were so successful that it was only a short time before he was able to give up medicine and concentrate entirely on literary activities. Interestingly, his very first contribution to *The Strand Magazine* didn't feature Sherlock Holmes, but was a piece entitled 'The Voice of Science', which appeared in March 1891 (it poked fun at the ladies' branch of the Eclectic Society, a fashionable scientific colloquium, which was exploring the properties of the phonograph or gramophone, which had been invented by Thomas Edison as recently as 1877).

The subject matter of 'The Voice of Science' underlined the fact that the late nineteenth century was a time not just of new ideas but also, more practically, of unprecedented advances in technology. These included innovations such as the motor car, Kodak camera and aeroplane, as well as new drugs, such as aspirin (1897), and medical techniques, notably X-rays, discovered by the German physicist Wilhelm Roentgen in 1895. Conan Doyle was an early adopter of all sorts of modern accessories (and was, in fact, one of the first people in Britain to receive a fine for speeding). But he seldom introduced them into his stories. There are only a few telephones in the canon (for example in the early story 'The Man with the Twisted Lip', published in December 1891), and only one reference to cars (in *His Last Bow*).

Despite the popular success of Sherlock Holmes, Conan Doyle put him in abeyance for most of the 1890s. A man of his restless curiosity could not be satisfied with churning out detective stories on a monthly basis. So, he appeared to kill off his consulting detective at the Reichenbach Falls (in 'The Final Problem', which appeared in *The Strand Magazine* in December 1893). He then turned his attention to new literary and scientific ventures. He travelled widely, often in search of healthier

climates for his wife, Louise, who had now been diagnosed with the dreaded tuberculosis. And, by the end of the century, he was in South Africa helping to run a field hospital in the Boer War, in which he had volunteered to serve militarily, but been rejected on account of his age.

He took this time to renew his interest in the study of the paranormal. In November 1893 he joined the Society for Psychical Research and the following spring he was in correspondence about spirit mediums with a prominent member, Professor Oliver Lodge, a hard-headed physicist, who combined an interest in this field with his discoveries of the capacity of electromagnetic wires to send messages without wires.

Conan Doyle responded with *The Parasite*, a novel about mesmerism, in December 1894. Mesmerism was a form of hypnotism or mind control which, because of its medical applications, was considered one of the more scientifically respectable areas of paranormal study. The book told of a young physiologist, Professor Gilroy, who fell under the spell of a female mesmerist, Miss Penclosa. Gilroy was a dogged materialist, with a credo, 'Show me what I can see with my microscope, cut with my scalpel, weigh in my balance, and I will devote a lifetime to its investigation'. But he was fascinated by Miss Penclosa's research which 'strikes at the very roots of life and the nature of the soul'. And he was particularly interested in what happened to the soul during mesmerism. When Gilroy's girlfriend was mesmerized, he noted, 'Her organs were acting – her heart, her lungs. But her soul! It had slipped from beyond our ken. Whither had it gone? What power had dispossessed it?'

The age-old clash between matter and spirit was not going away. Although it could be categorized as a religious debate, it also touched on several different aspects of science, including the growing study of the mind known as psychology. Here there was a similar division between the ideas of the Austrian neurologist Sigmund Freud and the British polymath Frederic Myers, a founder member (and, from 1900, President) of the Society for Psychical Research, of whom Conan Doyle was a strong admirer. On the one hand, in books such as *The Psychopathology of Everyday Life* (1901) and *Three Essays on The Theory of Sexuality* (1905), Freud advanced a materialist approach to the mind, and particularly the unconscious. Drawing on his studies with the French neurologist Jean-Martin Charcot into neurosis and hysteria, Freud firmly believed that mental problems had physical, i.e. material, causes. On the other hand, Myers – in his book *Human Personality and its Survival of Bodily Death* (1903) – put forward the case for the spiritual basis of personality (and the possibility of its continuance

Opposite A portrait of Thomas Edison (1847–1931) by Abraham Archibald Anderson (1847–1840).

Above Oliver Lodge (1851–1940), a prominent phyiscist in the field of radio, with whom Conan Doyle corresponded on the topic of the paranormal.

Above 'The Hound of the
Baskervilles', *a 1902 illustration
by Sidney Paget.*

after death). He was also interested in the unconscious, which he called the 'subliminal self', a function of the 'metetherial world' of images which ranged beyond the physical world. Significantly, when Conan Doyle wrote about his library in *Through the Magic Door* (1907), he took care to single out Myers's *Human Personality* as one of his favourite science volumes, one that he felt would grow in stature and be recognized in a century's time as 'a great root book, one from which a whole new branch of science will have sprung'.

Unencumbered for the time being by either Sherlock Holmes or daily medical practice, Conan Doyle was able to focus his mind on other branches of science. These came together in his complex Gothic-inspired novel *The Hound of the Baskervilles*, published in 1902. This pitches the forces of modern science, characterized by Sherlock Holmes, against powerful myths of the past, enshrined not just in the Baskerville family and the house and the moor they inhabit, but also in the fearful hound at the heart of the story. An essential part of the solution to the mystery comes when Holmes calls on Victorian ideas of heredity and genetics (as articulated by Francis Galton, an occasional correspondent of Conan Doyle) to suggest that Jack Stapleton, the agreeable naturalist who lives in the neighbourhood, is actually a Baskerville, and he is intent on using his vicious hound to kill Sir Henry Baskerville, the newly returned heir to the estate, and assuming the property for himself.

Galton was a cousin of Darwin, who expanded on the latter's ideas about natural selection to develop the non-science of eugenics (sometimes described as social Darwinism), which suggested that it might be possible, through the application of genetics, to weed out undesirable human characteristics and create a healthier and better race. This theory was linked to parallel concepts about degeneracy, which were part of the intellectual currency of the *fin de siècle* and which filtered into politics and the arts (mainly in attacks on the aesthetic movement). While not particularly sympathetic to such ideas himself, Conan Doyle allowed Sherlock Holmes to draw on criminological techniques linked to them – notably, as in *The Hound of the Baskervilles*, those of the Italian anthropologist Cesare Lombroso, who posited that certain criminals were born with inherited physical traits that condemned them atavistically to their anti-social behaviour.

By now, Conan Doyle was entering middle age; his own life was changing, and with it his attitudes to the world. In 1906 his wife Louise died. Her struggles with tuberculosis had influenced much of his activity until then. A couple of years later he moved with his new spouse, Jean Leckie, to Sussex, where an additional scientific interest occupied him – the search for prehistoric fossils in the Wealden clay not far from his house. This quest led him to expand his research into geology and anthropology, which all added to the bank of scientific knowledge that fed into his world view. One dig he was involved in was connected to the discovery of the Piltdown Man, a supposed prehistoric missing link, later found to be a hoax (and Conan Doyle was suspected as a perpetrator of the deception).

This pursuit coincided with a new departure in his writing – a series of books featuring the scientist Professor Challenger. The first of these, *The Lost World* (1912), told of a scientific expedition to South America to find a living dinosaur. This was still the age of exploration, and mounting such research-orientated journeys to the furthest parts of the world was an extension of the spirit of scientific enquiry.

By then Conan Doyle's personal commitment to scientific orthodoxy was wavering. He had tried to maintain his credibility as an objective scientist. But at the start of

Below A Discussion of the Piltdown Skull, *oil on canvas, by John Cooke (1866–1932).*

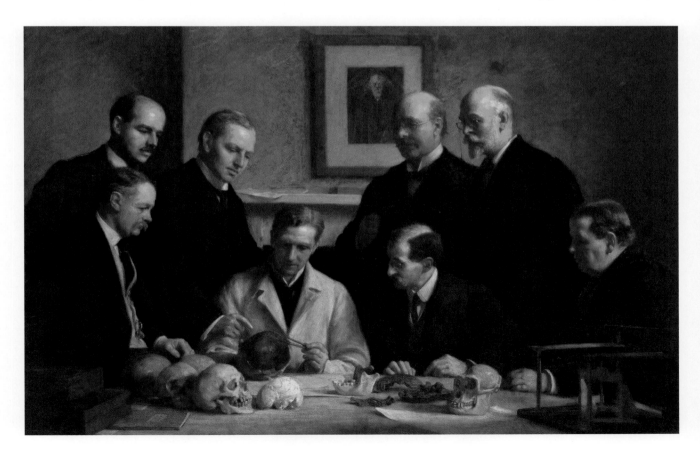

the First World War he found he could no longer retain his impartiality on issues of the spirit. He abandoned his carefully nurtured scepticism on such matters and became a fully-fledged spiritualist.

Thereafter his only quasi-scientific experiments were into the workings of séances and other manifestations of spiritualism, such as spirit photography. Perhaps his most misguided venture was his advocacy of the Cottingley Fairies, the images of supposed spirit forms which were faked by a couple of clever girls in Yorkshire.

In the last couple of decades of his life, he was no longer taken seriously as a public commentator on science, or, it must be admitted, anything much. In keeping with this, his two further Challenger books took on a mystical tone. But he made a point of ensuring that Sherlock Holmes maintained a rationalist view of the world. As late as 1924, when presented with evidence of paranormal activity in 'The Adventure of the Sussex Vampire', the detective dismisses any recourse to a supernatural intermediary, and declares, 'This Agency stands flat-footed upon the ground and there it must remain. The world is big enough for us. No ghosts need apply.' Conan Doyle may, by then, have been away

with the fairies, but he was smart enough to make sure that Sherlock Holmes maintained the tried and tested questing methodology which came from being a scientist.

Below One of the 1917 'Cottingley Fairies' photographs created by Frances Griffiths and Elsie Wright.

WATCHING THE
DETECTIVES

By around the year 1900, most people in Britain knew what a detective looked like. He was tall and gaunt, wore a deerstalker hat and sometimes a cape, smoked a curved pipe, and used a magnifying glass to help him with his investigations. It is true that the average hard-pressed investigator would have come across rather differently in reality. But this was how Sherlock Holmes, the fictional detective featured in Arthur Conan Doyle's stories, appeared. And his was the image that counted. By this time, or soon after, it was fixed in the minds of hundreds of thousands of people who read of his exploits in *The Strand Magazine*, illustrated by Sidney Paget, or who saw him portrayed on the stage by William Gillette.

Holmes represented the visible face of an intriguing public figure who had steadily emerged over the previous few decades – the probing sleuth whose job was to use a mixture of personal ingenuity and modern science to uncover the perpetrators of specific acts of criminality. The historical roots of this profession are much discussed. Some commentators look back to the Old Testament and point to Daniel's examination of the elders who had tried to rape Susanna. A more useful beginning is 1747, with the publication of Voltaire's novel *Zadig*, where

in an exemplary show of Enlightenment reasoning the eponymous Babylonian philosopher was able to describe the king's horse and the queen's dog from the physical marks they left behind. Seeing, observing and drawing the right conclusions were defining skills of any aspiring detective from the start.

Proper policing (as opposed to detection) took off in Britain at the same time as *Zadig*. The Bow Street Runners, the first officially sanctioned law enforcement agency, were founded in 1749 by the London magistrate (and novelist) Henry Fielding. Stories of criminals were initially much more popular than those of their pursuers. *The Newgate Calendar* comprised listings of felons' crimes, testimonies and executions, drawn up in 1774 by the Keeper of Newgate Prison, adjacent to the Central Criminal Court at the Old Bailey. It proved hugely successful, encouraging a range of publishers to expand this model into sensationalist accounts of the 'true stories' of notorious criminals and murderers, usually taken directly from legal trials. Conan Doyle is on record as having read and enjoyed them.

Writers subsequently became more ambitious and tried not just to engage their readers, but to startle them with fanciful literary concoctions, often described as 'Gothic'.

Written in this genre, Thomas de Quincey's essay 'On Murder Considered as One of the Fine Arts', published in 1827, equated murder with fashionably 'sublime' acts of the kind admired by contemporary Romantic poets and artists. De Quincey was influenced by a rash of violent crimes at the start of the century, particularly the Ratcliffe Highway Murders of 1811, when seven members from two separate families were killed.

The Bow Street Runners did not prove effective in protecting the public, so society was obliged to take firmer measures to protect both individuals and property. The founding of the Metropolitan Police in 1829, and of other provincial police forces soon after, had an immediate, beneficial effect on law and order.

Crime did not disappear, however; it became more sophisticated. No longer a matter of assaults in dark alleys, it entered the home and workplace. And when the bobby on the beat required professional support to keep up with the workload, detective departments were set up. The Met spawned a detective branch in 1842, though it had to wait another thirty-five years, until shortly before Sherlock Holmes, for a proper Criminal Investigation Department. One reason for this delay was that these new investigative

policemen were viewed with suspicion. They were regarded as intruders, an unwanted branch of the state, even the military. And if they tried to question anyone at home, this was a blatant invasion of privacy.

One person who continued to hold this view for another half-century was Dr Leslie Armstrong, a leading light in the medical school at Cambridge University. Holmes consulted Armstrong over the disappearance of his student Godfrey Staunton in 'The Adventure of the Missing Three-Quarter' (a story first published in August 1904 but usually said to be set in 1896). Armstrong told the detective dismissively, 'I am aware of your profession – one of which I by no means approve.'

Opposite 'Smith Stabbing a Policeman', illustration by Phiz for The New Newgate Calendar *by Camden Pelham (1841).*

Below The body of John Williams, perpetrator of the brutal Ratcliffe Highway Murders of 1811, is paraded through the streets of London.

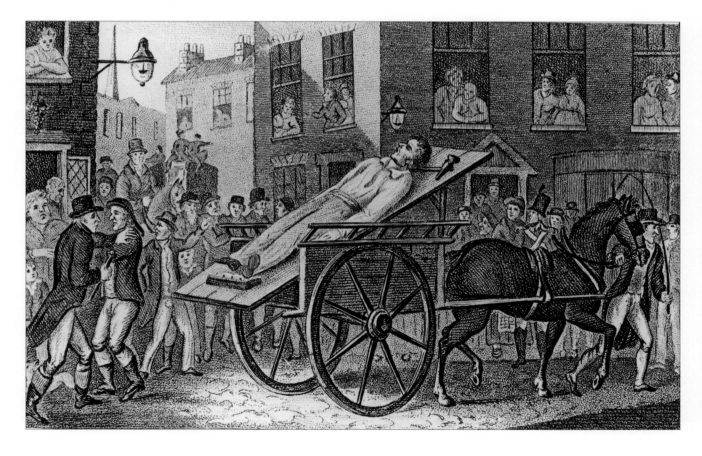

And he explains:

So far as your efforts are directed towards the
suppression of crime, sir, they must have the
support of every reasonable member of the
community, though I cannot doubt that the official
machinery is amply sufficient for the purpose.
Where your calling is more open to criticism is
when you pry into the secrets of private individuals,
when you rake up family matters which are better
hidden, and when you incidentally waste the time
of men who are more busy than yourself.

Holmes retorts that detectives such as himself actually
prevent the public airing of private matters in the way
that occurs when they fall into the hands of the police. He
describes himself as 'an irregular pioneer, who goes in front
of the regular forces of the country.'

By the middle of the nineteenth century detectives
were nevertheless making their mark on society. Tales of
detection were beginning to appear in fiction. They were
spurred on by a new kind of true-crime story, often written
by former policemen or lawyers. Particularly influential were
the memoirs of Eugène François Vidocq, published in 1827.
Vidocq was a former criminal who had headed the Paris
plain-clothes unit, the Sûreté nationale, during Napoleonic
times, and had later set up his own private investigation
agency, the Bureau des Renseignements. His reminiscences
inspired characters in the novels of many major French
authors, including Honoré de Balzac and Victor Hugo. They
also attracted a considerable following in Britain, where as
early as 1829 the hit play *Vidocq! The French Police Spy* was
running at the Coburg Theatre in London.

Elsewhere in Britain, Samuel Warren used his career
in the law as the source for a series of novels about the
English legal system. His book *Experiences of a Barrister* was
first published in 1852 in *Blackwood's Magazine*. Although
written well before his birth, this book was clearly familiar
to Conan Doyle, who mentioned two characters from it
(members of the legal profession called Ferret and Sharpe)
in his autobiography *Memories and Adventures*. There,
recalling how Holmes got his name, his creator wrote,
'One rebelled against the elementary art which gives some
inkling of character in the name, and creates Mr Sharps or
Mr Ferrets. First it was Sherringford Holmes; then it was
Sherlock Holmes.'

Simultaneously in 1852, the Scottish writer John Hill Burton published his *Narratives from Criminal Trials in Scotland*, a book which probably had a greater influence on the genesis of Sherlock Holmes than is generally acknowledged. Conan Doyle's mother, Mary, was a close friend of Hill Burton's wife, a formidable campaigner for women's rights and education. When his father was in an asylum suffering from alcoholism, the young Arthur went to live with the Hill Burtons at Liberton Bank in the Pentland Hills outside Edinburgh. His sister Lottie was born there, and his closest childhood companion was the Hill Burtons' son, William, who later worked in public health. In *Narratives from Criminal Trials in Scotland*, John, the father of the clan, comments shrewdly on the relationship between crime and science – and particularly how the former had failed to keep up with the latter. He wrote:

> One of the most observable things in the history of crime is the slowness with which it adopts, when it adopts at all, the aids of advancing science … All our great discoveries, from printing down to the electric telegraph, have aided in the detection, rather than the accomplishment of crime, and

every new surrender of physical difficulties to scientific skill gives the supporters of order and morality more checks on licentiousness and vice.

In pointing out how science always tends to be one step or more ahead of the criminal, Hill Burton undoubtedly put ideas in young Conan Doyle's head.

On a more popular level, William Russell, about whom little personal detail is known, penned a series of quasi-autobiographical stories (brought together as *The Recollections of a Policeman*) to *Chambers's Edinburgh Journal* between 1849 and 1852. He followed this up with *Recollections of a Detective Police-Officer* in 1856.

The first author to introduce an identifiable detective-type character into his fiction was the American Edgar Allan Poe. He created Auguste Dupin, a Parisian

Opposite 'Bow Street, and the Assembling of the Police', an illustration for The Penny Magazine, *31 January 1837.*

Below Newgate: Committed for Trial, *oil on canvas, by Frank Holl (1845–88).*

Above Portrait of Edgar Allan Poe
*(1809–49), American short story
writer and poet.*

Opposite Illustration by Arthur
*Rackham (1867–1939) for Edgar
Allen Poe's 'The Murders in the
Rue Morgue'.*

gentleman who loved solving puzzles, codes and mysteries, and who first appeared in Poe's story 'The Murders in the Rue Morgue', published in *Graham's Magazine* in Philadelphia in 1841. Anticipating Sherlock Holmes's often quirky scenarios, Dupin used his skills to conclude that these murders were committed by the unlikely figure of an orangutan. The story's narrator made clear that, although never described specifically as a detective, Dupin's unusual talent was analysis. But he stressed that this did not mean merely remembering things. Proper analysis required an extra dimension, elsewhere described as 'ratiocination': 'it is in matters beyond the limits of mere rule that the skill of the analyst is evinced. He makes in silence a host of observations and inferences.' And he succeeds through knowing what to observe – the quality which Dr Joseph Bell inculcated in the student Conan Doyle at Edinburgh University thirty years later and which Sherlock Holmes impressed on Dr Watson.

Dupin's exploits drew in part on those of the real-life Parisian policeman Eugène Vidocq. In 'The Murders in the Rue Morgue', Poe would dismiss Vidocq as 'a good guesser, and a persevering man. But, without educated thought, he erred continually by the very intensity of his investigations'. In this way he would anticipate Conan Doyle's disparaging references to both Dupin and Monsieur Lecoq (another French fictional character – a detective who first surfaced in 1866 in the novel *L'Affaire Lerouge* penned by Émile Gaboriau).

By this time, detectives had begun to appear in British novels. As an astute observer of society, Charles Dickens was particularly interested in their development. From 1850–51 he ran a series of articles in his newspaper *Household Words* about the Met's Detective Branch, including one titled 'On Duty with Inspector Field'. This featured the real-life Inspector Charles Frederick Field, who was subsequently the model for the tenacious fictional Inspector Bucket, who solved the mystery of Mr Tulkinghorn's in *Bleak House*, published 1852–53. (According to the Oxford English Dictionary, the first use of the word 'detective' as a noun was in this *Household Words* series, though it had appeared elsewhere in adjectival form in 1843.)

Household Words also wrote about Field's colleague, Inspector Jonathan Whicher, one of Scotland Yard's eight original detectives. Whicher became a victim of mid-century concerns about detectives invading the privacy of respectable English families when in 1860 he was called to investigate the brutal murder of a three-year-old boy

at Road Hill House in a country village near Frome in
Wiltshire. He identified the child's half-sister, Catherine
Kent, as the murderer. But this suggestion horrified the
Kent family, and Whicher was forced to return to
London with his reputation deflated. Catherine Kent
was originally acquitted of the murder, but later confessed
to the crime.

A similar fate befell Sergeant Cuff in Wilkie
Collins's novel, *The Moonstone*, published in 1868 and
often described as the first full-scale detective novel.
Only two years earlier Collins had reflected society's
ambivalence towards the detective in another novel
Armadale, where he had railed against the use of the
private detective, describing him as 'the vile creature
whom the viler need of Society has fashioned for its own
use … the Confidential Spy of modern times, whose
business is steadily enlarging, whose Private Inquiry
Offices are steadily on the increase.' In *The Moonstone*
Sergeant Cuff is portrayed more sympathetically as he
carries out a Whicher-type role – the London detective
sent to the provinces to add professional lustre to the
local constabulary's investigation. But his theory about
the disappearance of the jewel at the centre of the tale

proved wrong. And he too is unceremoniously asked to
leave the house where the crime occurred because of his
seemingly intrusive behaviour.

Detectives, in real life and in fiction, had caught the
imagination of the nation. They seemed to be everywhere.
In *The Moonstone* Gabriel Betteredge, the old family retainer
at the house where the supposed theft had occurred,
observes, 'Do you feel an uncomfortable heat at the pit of
your stomach, sir? And a nasty thumping at the top of your
head? … I call it the detective-fever; and I first caught it in
the company of Sergeant Cuff.'

Women detectives appeared – initially in Edward Ellis's
Ruth the Betrayer; or, The Female Spy, which appeared as a
penny dreadful in fifty-two parts from 1862–63, and then
in Andrew Forester's *The Female Detective* the following year.
The detective story was so widespread that it provoked a
backlash. In an essay in the *Saturday Review* in 1864, James
Fitzjames Stephen argued that 'this detective-worship
appears one of the silliest superstitions that ever were
concocted by ingenious writers.' Stephen did not like the
way in which fictional detectives assumed almost god-like
powers, which enabled them to visualize a whole sequence
of events from a single clue. He regarded this as guesswork

rather than the proper sifting of evidence which took place in a law court.

Into this world stepped Arthur Conan Doyle. There are details elsewhere about how he had absorbed some of the basic principles of detection during his time as a medical student at Edinburgh University. In particular, his Professor of Surgery Dr Joseph Bell drilled into him the importance of observation. He later thought to himself that if his old teacher were a detective, 'he would surely reduce this fascinating but unorganized business to something nearer to an exact science.' So, he decided to make Sherlock Holmes a scientific detective who truly mirrored his age.

But there were others who taught Conan Doyle at Edinburgh University who, in their own way, had as much influence as Bell in providing him with the scientific grounding that Holmes needed for his careful analysis and deduction. One was Professor Robert Christison, the Professor of Materia Medica and Therapeutics, an authority on forensic toxicology who had written books such as *A Treatise on Poisons and Medico-Legal Examination of Dead Bodies*. When lecturing about poisons and their origins in plants, one of Christison's classroom tricks was to demonstrate how indigenous South Americans fired curare, a toxic alkaloid,

from blowpipes. This may have inspired the Andaman Islander Tonga's favoured method of assassination in *The Sign of Four*. It was also behind the murderer Jefferson Hope's recollection in *A Study in Scarlet* of a professor who showed his students a deadly vegetable alkaloid which came directly from some South American arrow poison. Hope stole some of this toxin and worked it into small pills which he carried with him.

After Christison retired in 1877 (a year after Conan Doyle arrived at the university), he was followed by Professor Thomas Richard Fraser, who shifted the department's focus from anatomy to plants and practical pharmacology. The young Conan Doyle found himself spending hours researching the properties of various alkaloids, including gelsemium, which had uses (like curare) as a muscle relaxant, but which could also be lethal. He experimented with taking ever-larger doses of this drug, and wrote up his findings in a paper which he sent to the *British Medical Journal* where it appeared in September 1879, his first published work.

Conan Doyle channelled this interest in poisons into the Holmes stories. The first time the detective appears, in his laboratory at St Bartholomew's Hospital, he sticks a piece of plaster over a cut on his finger and remarks, 'I have to be careful for I dabble with poisons a good deal.' But even

Right Portrait of Sir Robert Christison (1871), one of Conan Doyle's teachers at Edinburgh University.

Opposite Indigenous tribespeople in Brazil hunting using sarbacanes (blowpipes) filled with poison to hunt for animals.

Holmes proves unfamiliar with the African root which Dr Leon Sterndale uses to murder his victims in 'The Adventure of the Devil's Foot'. Sterndale boasts that, 'save for one sample in a laboratory at Buda, there is no other specimen in Europe. It has not yet found its way either into the pharmacopoeia or into the literature of toxicology.'

Nevertheless, poisons were being increasingly used with murderous intent, and a good detective needed to know about them. According to one survey, out of eighty-three murder trials at the Old Bailey involving poison between 1739 and 1878, sixty-three took place after 1839. In another study of 540 cases of criminal poisoning between 1750 and 1914, 47 per cent involved arsenic (which had been identified by the English chemist James Marsh as recently as 1836), followed by opiates (10 per cent), strychnine (8 per cent) and acids (7 per cent). Even control of the sale of arsenic in the Arsenic Act of 1851 failed to halt this pattern of growth. So, it was useful for Holmes to be aware of poisons, but strangely, arsenic itself is not mentioned at all in the canon.

As with Tonga's blowpipe, poisons could be administered by puncturing someone's skin. The potential for this being used for criminal purposes increased in the early 1850s with the invention of the hypodermic syringe by the Scotsman Alexander Wood and, almost simultaneously, by the Frenchman Charles Pravez. But this doesn't seem to have been widely used as a murder weapon; in the canon, the syringe is most in evidence to aid Holmes's ingestion of cocaine.

The needle is sometimes used in this context as a signifier of Holmes. But he is more usually portrayed with those other accoutrements (mentioned earlier) which are in fact anachronisms. The consulting detective never wore a deerstalker hat or an Inverness cape in Conan Doyle's stories, nor did he smoke a calabash pipe. The deerstalker was an artistic invention of Sidney Paget who illustrated 'The Boscombe Valley Mystery' in *The Strand Magazine* in October 1891 with this piece of headgear, his interpretation of Conan Doyle's reference in the story to a 'close-fitting cloth cap'. There's another rendering of a deerstalker in Paget's illustration for 'The Adventure of Silver Blaze' in December the following year where an 'ear-flapped travelling-cap' is mentioned. But nowhere in the canon is a deerstalker cited or described. The cape Holmes is credited with donning in the stories is an Ulster, a fuller version of the Inverness, but with sleeves. The origin of the curved pipe is something of a mystery, said to be linked to

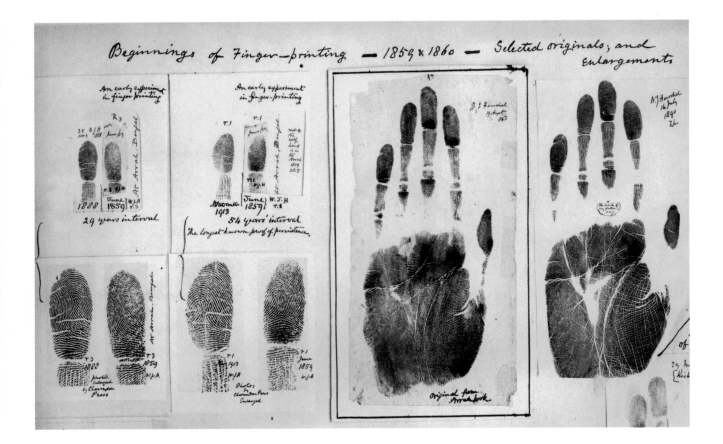

the way the American actor William Gillette portrayed the character on stage. Though known for his fondness for tobacco, which helped him address any 'three-pipe problem', the detective in the printed text only smokes through a straight clay, briar-root or cherry-wood pipe.

Holmes did, however, invariably use one item which is firmly associated with his public image – the magnifying glass, or lens. This crucial tool of his profession is there from the first time he visits a crime scene in *A Study in Scarlet*, published 1886–67: 'As he spoke, he whipped a tape measure and a large round magnifying glass from his pocket. With these two implements he trotted noiselessly about the room, sometimes stopping, occasionally kneeling, and once lying flat upon his face.' This vision of the detective at work endures. Holmes, as often noted, liked to observe, and a magnifying glass sometimes allowed him to do that even better than with the naked eye.

A decade and a half later, when 'The Adventure of the Norwood Builder' was published in 1903, the magnifying glass was still an obvious implement for a consulting detective of Holmes's scientific bent, and particularly so as an aid to the investigative technique of studying fingerprints. At that time, taking fingerprints had only

recently been officially introduced into the routine of the Metropolitan Police. It had been pioneered in India in the 1870s by Sir William Herschel, the chief magistrate of Hooghly, who used it to verify people's identities in a largely illiterate society. It was then developed by Charles Darwin's cousin, the polymath scientist Francis Galton, who in 1892 published an influential book *Finger Prints*, which set out a system of classification for the arches, loops and whorls of the average print. The establishment of Scotland Yard's fingerprint bureau followed in 1901, the year that Edward Henry, who had further refined the use of fingerprints in his police work in India, was appointed Assistant Commissioner in charge of the CID.

In 'The Adventure of the Norwood Builder', Holmes is invited by Inspector Lestrade of Scotland Yard to use a magnifying glass to inspect 'the well-marked print of a thumb' at a murder scene. Lestrade, who had no doubt been trained to look at fingerprints at the Yard, asks patronizingly, 'You are aware that no two thumb-marks are alike?' When Holmes replies, a little defensively, 'I have heard something of the kind,' the inspector demands. 'Well, then, will you please compare that print with this wax impression of young McFarlane's right thumb, taken

by my orders this morning?' When, according to the
story, the inspector holds up the waxen print close to the
bloodstain, 'it did not take a magnifying glass to see that
the two were undoubtedly from the same thumb.' Lestrade
opines, 'That is final', and Holmes cannot but agree, 'It
is final'. Although fingerprint evidence was still met with
scepticism by both professionals and the general public alike,
by 1905, only two years later, it was accepted as irrefutable
in securing the conviction and execution of the two Stratton
brothers who had murdered a paint shop owner in Deptford.

Conan Doyle was not the first author to incorporate
fingerprints into stories. In 1893 the American Mark Twain
used Galton's assertion that everyone's fingerprints are
different, even those of twins, to prove a point in a criminal
trial in his novel *Pudd'nhead Wilson: Those Extraordinary Twins*.
A few months earlier, Twain had written to his publisher
Chatto & Windus to express his delight at being sent a copy
of Galton's book, signing his letter with eight fingerprints.

To Sherlock Holmes, fingerprints were one of a favoured
type of clue – something involving a mark, print or sign,
bodily or otherwise. His job was to observe these 'trifles'
and draw the requisite conclusions. It was a practice he
worked hard at and wrote about, both in his stories and in
his monographs, which covered important aspects of his
craft such as 'secret writings' (ciphers, as in 'The Adventure
of the Dancing Men'), 'tattoo marks' ('The Red-Headed
League'), 'the ashes of 140 different varieties of pipe, cigar
and cigarette tobacco' ('The Boscombe Valley Mystery') and
several others.

In fact, fingerprints only play a peripheral and generally
inconclusive part in the Holmes stories, whereas footprints
are more central to the detective's investigations. This may
be largely because, as he recalled in *The Sign of Four*, he wrote
a monograph on 'the tracing of footsteps, with some remarks
upon the uses of plaster of Paris as a preserver of impresses'.
Amongst several detection techniques he calls on to solve
'The Boscombe Valley Mystery', he meticulously scours the
scene of a murder in
a remote wood, turning over leaves and dry sticks, gathering
samples of dust, and 'examining with his lens not only the
ground but even the bark of the tree as far as he could reach.'
Having inspected the boots of those present, he then analyzes
the footprints he finds in the wood. In 'The Adventure of
the Beryl Coronet' he is able to show, from what is described
as 'a very careful examination of the sill with his powerful
magnifying glass', how Arthur Holder had exited a window
from his father Alexander's house in his bare feet in pursuit

*Opposite Fingerprints taken by
Sir William Herschel in 1859
and 1860.*

*Above 'Look at that with your
magnifying glass, Mr Holmes',
a 1911 illustration by Sidney
Paget for 'The Adventure of the
Norwood Builder'.*

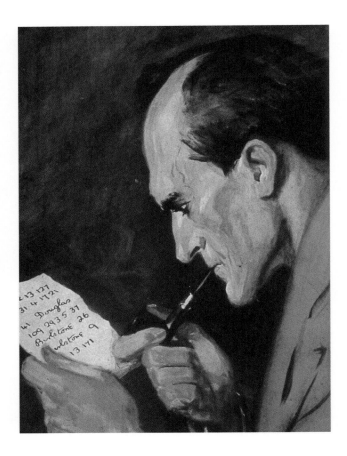

of his friend Sir George Burnwell who has stolen the coronet
at the centre of the story. Holmes also demonstrates from the
cover of snow on the ground that the shoes of the man waiting
outside the window to be passed the coronet by his lover Mary
Holder, the niece of Alexander Holder, was indeed Sir George,
her lover.

For all his pretensions to being scientific, Holmes normally
opted for low-tech aids to detection, such as analysis of
handwriting. When he asked Watson in *The Sign of Four* if he
had 'ever had occasion to study character in handwriting', he
was mulling over the letter sent to his new client Miss Morstan,
who would later marry Watson. When the Doctor replied
that the writing was legible and regular, showing someone
businesslike and forceful, Holmes disagreed strongly, declaring,
'Look at his long letters … They hardly rise above the common
herd. That d might be an a, and that i an e. Men of character
always differentiate their long letters, however illegibly they
may write. There is vacillation in his ks and self-esteem in
his capitals.'

Today the consensus is that graphology is not a science.
But, in keeping with the enquiring spirit of the age, there was
considerable interest in its possibilities in the late nineteenth
century. In France, the French priest and archaeologist
Jean-Hippolyte Michon published *Système de graphologie* in
1875 and *Méthode pratique de graphologie* three years later. His
compatriot Jules Crépieux-Jamin would offer graphological
evidence at the trial of Alfred Dreyfus in 1895. They both
argued that handwriting could point to human personality traits.

Holmes tended towards this opinion. He suggested at
different times that an individual's script could help determine
age, gender, health and even nationality. In 'The Adventure
of the Reigate Squire' he divined from a scrap of a letter that
it was composed by two people, writing alternate words, and
that they were blood relatives, thus managing to implicate the
Cunningham brothers who lived nearby. (He admitted that this
was only one of twenty-three deductions he could have made,
but the others would only really interest experts in the field.)

As an extension of this skill Holmes was good at discerning
significant information from typewritten texts. Having stated
his intention to add to his corpus of monographs with one
on 'The typewriter and its relation to crime', he is easily able
in 'A Case of Identity' to expose James Windibank's bizarre
attempts to impersonate his stepdaughter's would-be fiancé
Hosmer Angel. Holmes does this by comparing Windibank's
typewritten letter with those from Angel. He remarks, 'A
typewriter has really quite as much individuality as a man's
handwriting. Unless they are quite new, no two of them write

exactly alike. Some letters get more worn than others, and some wear only on one side.'

He also has a useful, if esoteric, line in working out the origins of specific pieces of newspaper text. In *The Hound of the Baskervilles*, he trumpets this 'special hobby', claiming there was as much difference between 'the leaded bourgeois type of a *Times* article and the slovenly print of an evening half-penny paper' as between a Black man and an Eskimo. Uncharacteristically, he admits to once when 'very young' confusing the *Leeds Mercury* with the *Western Morning News*. 'But a *Times* leader is entirely distinctive.'

Among Holmes's other talents as a detective were reading ciphers (best demonstrated in 'The Adventure of the Dancing Men'), analyzing documents, and, more esoterically, interpreting canine behaviour. In 'The Adventure of the Creeping Man' he reveals his intention to write yet another monograph: *'Upon the Uses of Dogs in the Work of the Detective'*. He suggests that one can predict the behaviour of humans from their animals. He explains that he has come to a similar conclusion about families – and how it is possible from 'the mind of the child, to form a deduction as to the criminal habits of the very smug and respectable father.' Famously in 'The Adventure of Silver Blaze' he was able to determine the

course of events at Colonel Ross's stables by observing how the dog had not reacted. When Inspector Gregory, a rising star among Scotland Yard's detectives, notes that the dog had done nothing in the night-time, Sherlock Holmes replies, 'That was the curious incident.'

Surprisingly, Holmes does not give much credence to photographs in reaching his conclusions. They are not part of his detective's bag of tricks. They are mentioned in passing; for example, providing the evidence of the attempted blackmail at the heart of 'A Scandal in Bohemia'. But no police snapper ever appears at a crime scene.

And he pays only lip service to other modish attempts at charting criminal behaviour, most of which had been pioneered in Europe. Best known was anthropometrics, which had been invented in the early 1880s by the rootless French academic, Alphonse Bertillon. The main idea was that you could measure certain parts of the body, notably the head, and use the results to compare and even predict criminal behaviour. From 1884, the Paris police began to group photographs of criminals not by alphabet, but by measurement of eleven essential features. They reported success in identifying recidivists, and four years later formed a Department of Judicial Identity under Bertillon. The

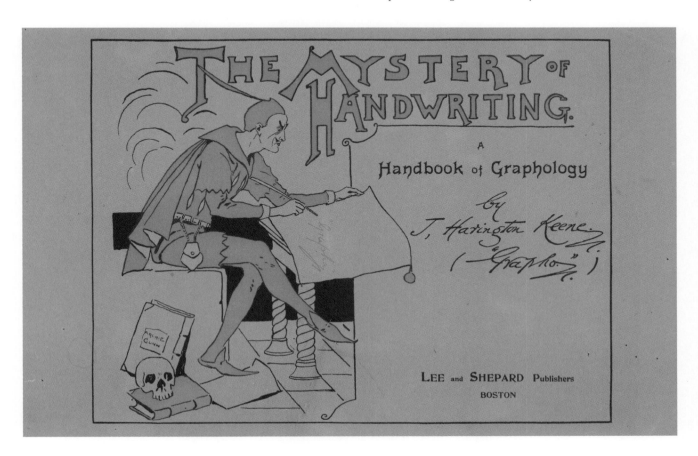

THE MYSTERY OF HANDWRITING.

A

Handbook of Graphology

by

J. Harington Keene

("Graphos").

LEE and SHEPARD Publishers

BOSTON

Metropolitan Police in London followed suit in 1894. But the system was found to be inferior to fingerprints, and Bertillon's reputation was not enhanced by his flawed testimony, which led to the conviction of the alleged German spy Captain Alfred Dreyfus in Paris that same year.

At one stage, travelling together to Woking in 'The Adventure of the Naval Treaty' (published in 1893), Watson records Holmes as expressing his 'enthusiastic admiration' for the works of Bertillon. But on the other occasion the Frenchman is mentioned in the canon, in *The Hound of the Baskervilles* (published later, in 1902), Holmes takes umbrage when Dr James Mortimer suggests he might only be the second-best authority on predicting behaviour from the examination of a skull. He is not impressed when Mortimer admits to having regarded Bertillon as top of the league, and the medical doctor doesn't exactly help his argument when he indicates that this was only his assessment as a 'man of precisely scientific mind'.

Around the same time, the Italian criminologist Cesare Lombroso addressed similar matters with a broader brush, arguing in his book *Criminal Man* (published 1876) that it was possible to identify a propensity to delinquency from a person's features, such as large jaws or fleshy lips. Such emphasis on

appearance brought certain practical developments in detection, such as the use of the police mugshot. Again, Holmes showed interest, most explicitly in his comments on Miss Cushing's ear in 'The Adventure of the Cardboard Box' when he lectures his companion:

> As a medical man, you are aware, Watson, that there is no part of the body which varies so much as the human ear. Each ear is as a rule quite distinctive and differs from all other ones. In last year's *Anthropological Journal* you will find two short monographs from my pen upon the subject. I had, therefore, examined the ears in the box with the eyes of an expert and had carefully noted their anatomical peculiarities. Imagine my surprise, then, when on looking at Miss Cushing I perceived that her ear corresponded exactly with the female ear which I had just inspected. The matter was entirely beyond coincidence. There was the same shortening of the pinna, the same broad curve of the upper lobe, the same convolution of the inner cartilage. In all essentials it was the same ear.

There are also elements of Lombroso in Holmes's deduction that Jack Stapleton, the naturalist at the other side of the moor,

is related to the Baskervilles. The detective demonstrates the similarity between Stapleton and the subject of one of the family portraits at Baskerville Hall. He tells Watson:

> My eyes have been trained to examine faces and not their trimmings. It is the first quality of a criminal investigator that he should see through a disguise … it is an interesting instance of a throwback, which appears to be both physical and spiritual. A study of family portraits is enough to convert a man to the doctrine of reincarnation. The fellow is a Baskerville – that is evident.

Holmes was getting carried away with his references to reincarnation, anticipating Conan Doyle's conversion to spiritualism during the First World War. But the detective was clearly interested in heredity as a guiding principle in nature. He made this clear in 'The Adventure of the Greek Interpreter' where he tells Watson that his powers of observation and deduction are hereditary rather than acquired skills. He mentions his links to the French artistic family of Vernet in support of the former claim and his relationship to his gifted brother Mycroft of the latter. But he doesn't anywhere subscribe to Lombroso's extreme ideas, which combine Darwinian concepts of the survival of the fittest with eugenics and racial profiling, and consequently have never become part of mainstream detection.

Nevertheless, Holmes was clearly aware that a new category of scientific enquiry called forensics was developing and liked to be ahead of the game where matters of detection were involved. When first introduced in the laboratory in St Bartholomew's Hospital, he is working on a test for blood stains which he claims will be the 'most practical medico-legal discovery for years'. It involves the discovery of a re-agent which is precipitated by haemoglobin; he goes on to explain the simple procedure, which involves mixing a small sample of blood to a litre (1¾ pints) of water and adding some unspecified crystals. Holmes says this will supersede any existing techniques, adding that the old guaiacum test was clumsy and uncertain, as is the microscopic examination of blood corpuscles, certainly of stains more than a few hours

"HOLMES WAS WORKING HARD OVER A CHEMICAL INVESTIGATION."

old. But his test will get results in perpetuity, showing if stains come from blood, mud, rust, fruit or anything else.

Strangely, nothing much came of the test and it is not mentioned again. No microscope is involved. This instrument only appears in two of his adventures: in 'The Adventure of Shoscombe Old Place', where Holmes uses a 'low power' microscope and boasts of having encouraged Scotland Yard to adopt more of them, and also in 'The Adventure of the Three Garridebs' where Nelson Garrideb appears to own a state-of-the-art version.

The Holmes test shows Conan Doyle's mind conjuring up a notable piece of science fiction. It anticipated by more than a decade the next main breakthroughs in the analysis of blood – the Austrian Karl Landsteiner's discovery of blood groups and the German bacteriologist Paul Uhlenhuth's antigen-antibody precipitin test (which enabled scientists to determine the species of a blood sample, confirming if it came from a human or an animal, along the lines Holmes had suggested). It also pointed the way to more sophisticated analysis in criminal cases of blood, urine, tissues, cells and other biospecimens, including DNA profiling or 'genetic fingerprinting' in the 1990s.

Having developed this range of expertise, Holmes tended to be grudging about the skills of the other professional detectives he meets. Or rather, he uses them preeningly to establish his pre-eminence as the world's only 'consulting detective'. (It's a similar story to his cursory acknowledgement of working scientists, as noted in the previous chapter.) In all, according to James O'Brien, twenty-one different detectives appear in forty-two of the sixty stories. Holmes deals most often with Inspector Lestrade of Scotland Yard, who appears in thirteen of the stories. Holmes describes him and his colleague Inspector Gregson as 'the pick of a bad lot' at the Yard. 'They are both quick and energetic' he concedes, but he can't help adding that they are also 'conventional – shockingly so.' His generally dismissive attitude is clear at the start of *A Study in Scarlet* where Gregson tells him proudly that he has left everything at the murder scene untouched, and Holmes

Opposite 'Holmes was working hard over a chemical investigation', an 1892 illustration by Sidney Paget for The Adventures of Sherlock Holmes.

Below An 1890 engraving of New Scotland Yard on the Thames Embankment, which served as headquarters for the Metropolitan Police from 1890–1967.

Above Edward Richard Henry
*(1850–1931), whose fingerprinting
system was adopted by Scotland
Yard in 1901.*

Opposite The Black Museum at
Scotland Yard in 1883.

points to the pathway and replies, 'If a herd of buffaloes had passed along, there could not be a greater mess.' And, just to emphasize the difference between this publicly appointed crew and an independent operator like himself, he continues, 'They have their knives into one another, too. They are as jealous as a pair of professional beauties.'

Holmes's general complaint is that the plods of Scotland Yard lack the vision and creativity that, by implication, he himself has. He is happy to admit that Inspector Gregory, whom he encountered in 'The Adventure of Silver Blaze' (1892), was an 'extremely competent officer'. But he couldn't help adding, 'Were he but gifted with imagination he might rise to great heights in his profession.'

His attitude to his professional rivals did, however, become more relaxed as the years rolled by. By *The Hound of the Baskervilles* (1902), Lestrade is 'the best of the professionals', whose observations are 'very good' by the time of 'The Adventure of the Bruce-Partington Plans' (1908). In 'The Adventure of the Golden Pince-Nez' (1904), Holmes commended Scotland Yard's Inspector Stanley Hopkins as 'a promising detective'. He also liked the Scots-born Inspector Macdonald who features in *The Valley of Fear* (1915), which shows how police forces work outside London and manage to cooperate with the Met. White Mason, the able Sussex detective in this story, had originally been informed of the murder at Birlstone Manor at three o'clock in the morning by the local village policeman, Sergeant Wilson, who had driven to see him in a light dogcart. Described as 'a quiet, comfortable-looking person in a loose tweed suit, with a clean-shaved, ruddy face, a stoutish body, and powerful bandy legs adorned with gaiters, looking like a small farmer, a retired gamekeeper, or anything upon earth except a very favourable specimen of the provincial criminal officer', White Mason had rushed to the scene of the crime and been able to forward details to Scotland Yard on the 5.40 a.m. train, allowing Macdonald and Holmes to meet and to travel down there by mid-day. The Sussex detective further demonstrated his nous by alerting his colleagues to the interest the case would arouse in the press – a fact of life which the police had, by that date, to deal with on a regular basis, but which, mercifully, did not affect the solitary freelance operator, Holmes.

In taking this equivocal attitude to his professional colleagues, or at least to those in public employment, Holmes was mirroring his creator, whose own links with the Metropolitan Police were cursory. Conan Doyle didn't get on with Colonel Sir Edward Bradford, the prickly former

Indian administrator with an amputated left arm, who was Scotland Yard's Commissioner for most of the 1890s. And he had little to do with Bradford's successor, Sir Edward Henry, another veteran of the Indian police service, who worked to introduce fingerprints into the Met. He did have one ally in the Met, however – Superintendent William Melville, head of Scotland Yard's Special Branch, who led the police fight against anarchists and terrorists in the last two decades of the century. When Melville retired in 1904, Conan Doyle lent his name to a committee seeking funds for a testimonial for the Superintendent. Melville later became chief of MO3, the counter-intelligence branch of military intelligence, before rising to head MI5, or the Security Service. This suggests that Conan Doyle was closer to the secret than the criminal investigation side of Scotland Yard's activities. In this respect, he was more like Mycroft than Sherlock Holmes.

However, more mundanely, Conan Doyle did, in 1892, accompany some friends to Scotland Yard's Black Museum, where a collection of bizarre exhibits and death masks from crime cases were kept. (In 'The Adventure of the Empty House' Watson remarks that the airgun assembled by the blind German, Von Herder, for Professor Moriarty's

sidekick, Colonel Sebastian Moran, will end up there.) And in 1901 Conan Doyle lobbied Scotland Yard to investigate an obscure case in Canada on behalf of his friend Cuthbert Whitaker, whose family firm produced the Almanacs used by the detective to read the cipher message sent to him at the start of *The Valley of Fear* about the impending murder at Birlstone.

When, after the turn of the century, Scotland Yard began extending its range of crime-solving techniques, Conan Doyle showed more interest, particularly with the new emphasis placed on forensic medicine. The Home Office worked closely with pathologists and toxicologists from London's St Mary's Hospital, one of whom, Bernard Spilsbury, would become famous for his courtroom involvement. Conan Doyle would get to know Spilsbury through his occasional involvement in 'Our Society', otherwise known as the 'Crimes Club', where writers and lawyers would meet to discuss interesting trials.

Conan Doyle was more relaxed with foreign policemen. Before the First World War, he befriended the American William J. Burns, a former Pinkerton's detective who had left that agency and set up his own. Burns was almost certainly Conan Doyle's source for his information on the

108 WATCHING THE DETECTIVES

Molly Maguires in *The Valley of Fear*. They shared the same US publisher, George H. Doran, and Burns had visited the British author at his home in Sussex in April 1913, shortly after his own book, *The Masked War: The Story of a Peril that Threatened the United States by the Man who Uncovered the Dynamite Conspirators and Sent Them to Jail*, appeared. When Conan Doyle passed through New York on two occasions after the war, Burns was on hand to help him on his way.

Travelling back from Australia by ship in early 1921, Conan Doyle made a point of disembarking at Marseilles and making his way back to England through France, and particularly Lyon, where he visited Dr Edmond Locard, who was often dubbed the French Sherlock Holmes. Locard had set up the first dedicated police forensics laboratory in Lyon in 1910. He had expanded the science of fingerprints and formulated the Locard principle of transfer (much lauded in the annals of detection), which stated that there is always a trace when two bodies come into contact. His work attracted considerable international interest; it seems that the young Belgian detective-story writer, Georges Simenon, visited him at much the same time. Conan Doyle was in fact directed to Locard by an unusually colourful friend

called Harry Ashton-Wolfe who, after a peripatetic career in the American West, had worked as an assistant to Alphonse Bertillon, the great advocate of criminal anthropometrics. Ashton-Wolfe went on to pen a series of garish detective novels, as well as drawing on his varied career for non-fiction titles such as *The Invisible Web: Strange Tales of the French Sûreté, etc*, published by Hurst and Blackett in 1928.

Inevitably, Conan Doyle's own help was sought to take up real-life cases, particularly where there had been a miscarriage of justice. He was generally reluctant to do this, though in early 1901, shortly before returning to writing about Sherlock Holmes in *The Hound of the Baskervilles*, he penned a series of true-crime stories titled 'Strange Studies from Life' for *The Strand Magazine*. But he was dissatisfied with the outcome of tales like 'The Debatable Case of Mrs Emsley', about the murder of a wealthy widow in London's East End, and soon discontinued them. He was more interested in trying to verify claims of ghostly or extra-sensory activity. In 1894 that fascination took him down to Charmouth in Dorset, with a couple of members of the Society for Psychical Research, to conduct an inconclusive investigation into reports of poltergeist activity.

Opposite 'The Bull's-Eye', by Gustave Doré, from London, a Pilgrimage *(1872), by William Blanchard Jerrold.*

Right Nineteenth-century advertisement for Pinkerton's National Detective Agency.

Geo. E.F. Edalji   3460 30·9·03

Above The police mugshot of George
Edalji, dated 30 September 1903.

Opposite The trial of Oscar Slater,
1 March 1909.

On two occasions, Conan Doyle relented and agreed to
add his own personal sleuthing skills to those of the police.
In November 1906 he was approached by George Edalji, a
half-Indian lawyer who was seeking a pardon after having
been convicted and imprisoned for three years for maiming
animals in the fields around where he lived in Great Wyrley
in Staffordshire. Conan Doyle met him in the Grand Hotel,
Charing Cross, and was immediately struck by the myopic
way in which Edalji read his newspaper. Having some training
in ophthalmology, he had some understanding of eyes, and
was convinced that there was no way this young man could
have committed the crimes in the middle of the night in the
way he was accused of. So, Conan Doyle set about lobbying
the Chief Constable of Staffordshire, Captain George Anson,
even taking his grievance to the Home Office. (Anson believed
that Edalji's bulging eyes and dark appearance identified him
as a potential criminal, according to the classifications of the
Italian criminologist Cesare Lombroso.) Conan Doyle also
used his access to the press to highlight what had happened,
even visiting the Home Secretary Herbert Gladstone to discuss
the details. Eventually, in May 1908, Edalji was exonerated,
but not paid any compensation. However, the case did
contribute to the setting up of the Court of Criminal Appeal

and Conan Doyle was able to give a talk to the Crimes Club to discuss what had passed.

Four years later, Conan Doyle took up another apparent judicial failing, the conviction on flimsy evidence of Oscar Slater for murder in Glasgow. Slater, a petty criminal, had been sentenced to hang, later commuted to penal servitude 'for the term of his natural life'. Conan Doyle wrote a supportive pamphlet – 'The Case of Oscar Slater' – and argued widely for a reprieve. When a Scottish journalist came up with evidence that the investigation had been badly bungled, Slater was released on licence. But by that time it was 1927, and he had been incarcerated for nearly two decades. When he sought to appeal against his original conviction, Conan Doyle chipped in with a £1,000 contribution. After Slater was granted £6,000 in compensation, Conan Doyle felt he should be reimbursed, leading to acrimonious exchanges between the two as the now-freed man refused.

Conan Doyle wasn't the only fiction writer to observe the rise of the detective and think they would make good subject matter. The general scamper to write detective fiction grew more intense after Sherlock Holmes was withdrawn from the ring (temporarily, as it turned out) in 1893, because of his apparent demise at the Reichenbach Falls. One of Conan Doyle's competitors was his own brother-in-law, E.W. Hornung, who, in 1898, invented the gentleman thief, A.J. Raffles, who had his own Watson-like companion, Bunny Manders. Conan Doyle appreciated these easily digested stories, but called them an inversion of Sherlock Holmes, and advised Hornung that a thief could not be a hero.

More strictly in the detective-story genre were: Arthur Morrison's sleuth Martin Hewitt, who quickly took up the column inches vacated by Homes in *The Strand Magazine*; Guy Boothby's sinister Dr Nikola, who appeared in the *Windsor Magazine*; and Cutcliffe Hyne's Captain Kettle, who chased after felons in *Pearson's Magazine*. Another dabbler in the art of creating sleuths was Grant Allen, who was Conan Doyle's neighbour in Surrey. When Allen, best known as a science writer, died in 1899, Conan Doyle agreed to finish the final two instalments of *Hilda Wade*, a Holmesian-inspired novel featuring an eponymous female detective, which his neighbour had been writing for *The Strand Magazine*.

Other countries produced similar detective stories, often in the Sherlockian mode, such as the exploits of Arsène Lupin, which appeared in France in 1905 from the

pen of Maurice Leblanc. When, the following year, another Lupin tale appeared with the title *Sherlock Holmes Arrives too Late*, Conan Doyle called in his lawyers, causing Leblanc to alter the name to Herlock Sholmes. The Frenchman proved obdurate, producing a volume in 1908 uncompromisingly titled *Arsène Lupin contre Herlock Sholmes*, which was later turned into a film.

Thereafter, detective stories proliferated, leading after the First World War to the so-called 'golden age' of crime fiction, which featured murder mysteries set in country houses and played to elaborate rules codified in 1929 by the Sherlockian Ronald Knox as the 'Ten Commandments'. Four of the best-known authors of this stylized genre were women – the 'queens of crime', Agatha Christie, Dorothy Sayers, Ngaio Marsh and Margery Allingham. Christie's career had kicked off with her publication of *The Mysterious Affair at Styles* in 1920.

By then, the business of detection had shifted subtly from the nineteenth-century style of scientific enquiry to a version of the twentieth-century science of psychology. Poirot likes to sit still in a chair and use his 'little grey cells'. As he rashly stated in *Five Little Pigs*, 'I do not need to bend and measure the footprints and pick up the cigarette ends and examine the bent blades of grass. It is enough for me to sit back in my chair and think.' Holmes did that too; there are many descriptions of him pondering over cases in his velvet-lined armchair. But he was good at the groundwork as well.

Right Hercule Poirot, here portrayed by David Suchet, did more of his detection work from the comfort of his armchair.

SCREEN AND STAGE REPRESENTATIONS

Sherlock Holmes and the cinema are much the same age. Although the detective had already featured in a couple of short novels, he first made his mark on the world in the monthly stories which appeared in *The Strand Magazine* from 1891. That same year the American Thomas Edison invented the Kinetoscope, the forerunner of the moving-picture projector. The Kinetoscope was then developed by the French Lumière brothers into the more user-friendly Cinématographe, the first real projector, which four years later was showing film to the general public and very soon after entertaining audiences around the world.

Conan Doyle never mentioned film or the cinema in the Sherlock Holmes stories. This is surprising as he liked new technical gadgets. He himself was an early adopter of the home-movie camera (several of his personal films from the 1920s can be found on the internet). But, although he must have been asked, he steered clear of rushing Sherlock Holmes onto the cinema screen.

For a while, Anglophone audiences had to make do with Holmes on Conan Doyle's preferred medium – the stage, initially as interpreted by the restrained but charismatic American actor William Gillette. The Yale-educated son of former US senator, Gillette had enjoyed a

considerable boost to his career when he teamed up with the impresario Charles Frohman to star in the American Civil War drama *Secret Service*, a play about a spy in the American civil war, which was a hit on both sides of the Atlantic in 1896–97.

Having managed to kill off Sherlock Holmes at the Reichenbach Falls in 1893, Conan Doyle was looking for a new revenue stream, and thought he might find it in the theatre. With the help of the actor-manager Henry Irving, he had already enjoyed some success with *A Straggler of '15*, his play about a veteran of Waterloo. So, later in the decade, he began thinking about a stage adaptation of his Holmes stories. He talked about this with another leading British impresario, Herbert Beerbohm Tree, but their discussions came to nothing. However, news of Conan Doyle's ambitions in this direction came to the attention of Charles Frohman when he brought *Secret Service* to the Garrick Theatre in London with its author Gillette in the lead.

The two Americans secured Conan Doyle's permission to bring Holmes to the stage. Gillette, who was to be responsible for the text of the adaptation, was given a free hand to do what he wanted with the stories. There was only one stipulation: initially, Conan Doyle did not want Holmes

Above Sherlock Holmes as played on the London Stage by William Gillette *(1907), watercolour by Leslie Ward (1851–1922).*

Opposite An 1899 poster advertising a stage adaptation of Sherlock Holmes starring William Gillette.

involved in any romantic interest. However, he relented on this, informing Gillette, as he later wrote in *The Strand Magazine*, that he could 'marry the detective, or murder him, or do anything he pleased with him, preferring to leave a stage detective in the hands of a master actor'.

The project started badly when the only version of Gillette's script was destroyed in a fire at San Francisco's Baldwin's Hotel and Theatre where he was playing *Secret Service*. He rewrote it from scratch, and the following spring took it to London to discuss with Conan Doyle. Having been given the go-ahead, a copyright performance was given at the Duke of York's Theatre in London on 12 June 1899. The première was at the Star Theatre in Buffalo on 23 October, leading, after a short tour, to a spectacularly successful run at the Garrick Theatre on Broadway in New York.

While drawing on elements from 'A Scandal in Bohemia', 'The Final Problem' and *A Study in Scarlet*, Gillette had taken liberties with the text, introducing a love interest in the character of Alice Faulkner, who was based on Irene Adler, and creating a new character called Billy the pageboy, who had been unnamed in Conan Doyle's stories. He also gave the detective a number of characteristics and stage props which would be associated with Holmes for evermore. One was his use of the phrase, 'Oh, this is elementary, my dear Watson,' which was adopted and shortened when Holmes came to the cinema screen. Furthermore, Gillette's Holmes regularly appeared with a curved briar-wood pipe (or calabash) to hand. This apparently made it easier for him to speak his words than an ordinary straight pipe. He also introduced a couple of important sartorial details – the long Inverness cape and, crucially, the deerstalker hat which, although it had already been pictured by Sidney Paget (the original illustrator of the stories), had not been specifically described by Conan Doyle. Such accessories were integral to his performance and to the enduring image of Sherlock Holmes.

The play *Sherlock Holmes* was a huge success, enjoying a run of 235 performances in New York before moving to London where it opened at the Lyceum Theatre on 9 September 1901, later transferring to the Duke of York's Theatre. A 1905 revival featured the young Charlie Chaplin as Billy the pageboy. Frohman would be killed when the liner the *Lusitania* was sunk by a German U-boat in 1915. But, despite regular interruptions for other productions, Gillette continued to play Holmes throughout his life, clocking up more than 1,300 appearances in the role, including a final tour in 1929 when he was seventy-six. By

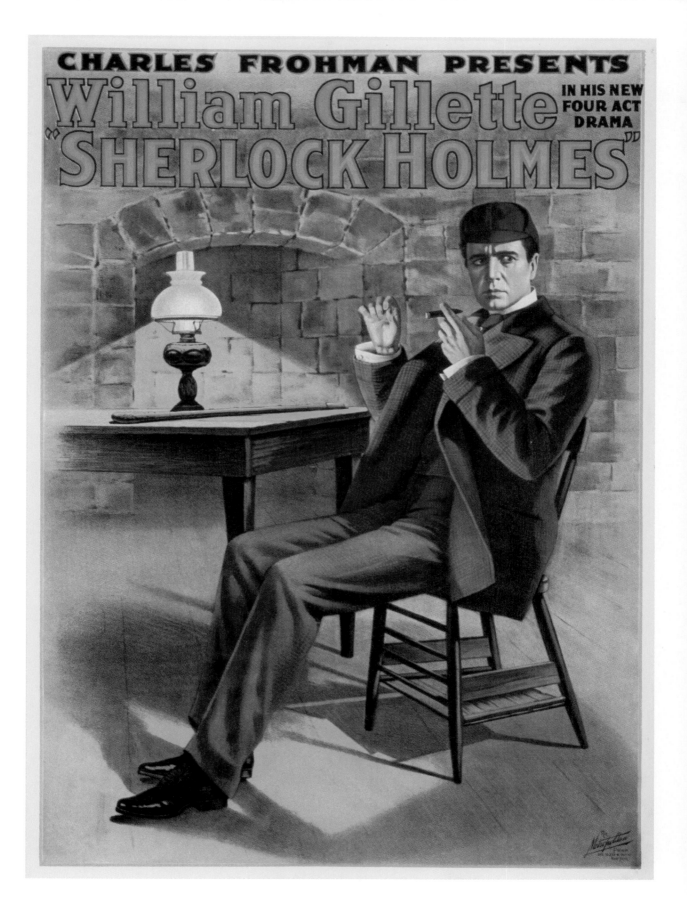

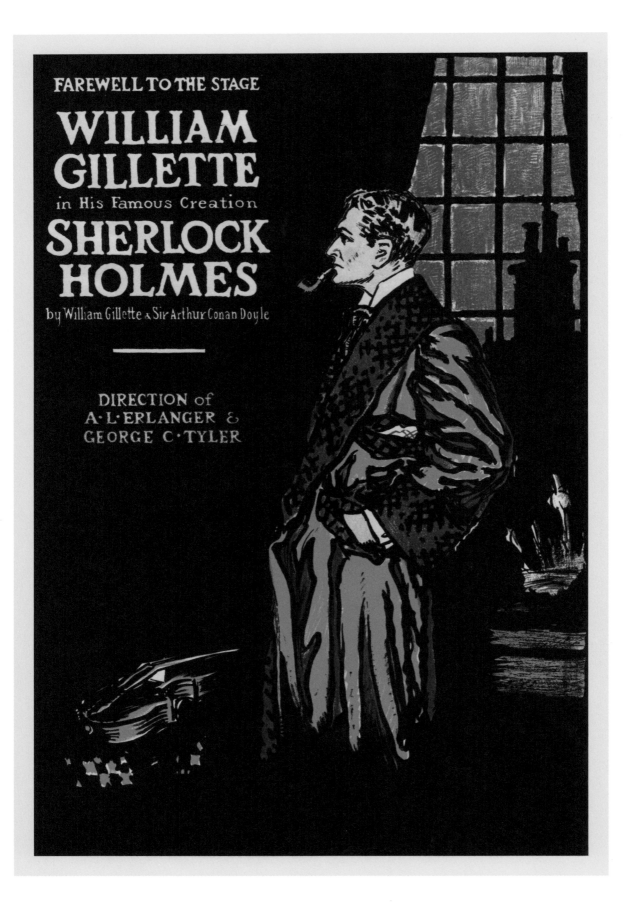

that time the role had made him a considerable fortune, part of which he ploughed into building a castle, complete with a narrow-gauge railway, on his 184-acre (75-hectare) estate in his native Connecticut, where he died in 1937 at the age of eighty-three.

By then Sherlock Holmes had been enthusiastically taken up by the cinema. Gillette had established the model for the detective's portrayal on both stage and film. However, he had little influence on the first flickering images of Holmes which had appeared in a very short (30-second) feature called *Sherlock Holmes Baffled*, made in 1900 by the American Mutoscope and Biograph Company. Using a cinematographic technique close to the old-fashioned flip book, the film shows Holmes surprising a burglar who then disappears leaving him 'baffled'. Although probably inspired by Gillette's success on stage, it has none of his sartorial or other effects.

Thereafter Scandinavia temporarily became the unexpected production hub for Holmes films. In Denmark the Nordisk Company in Copenhagen, a pioneer in silent movies, turned out eleven motion pictures, mostly starring Viggo Larsen in the title role, from 1908 to 1911, beginning with *Sherlock Holmes in Danger*. Larsen moved to Germany,

Opposite A 1929 poster advertising William Gillette's final performance as the great detective, by which time he was seventy-six years old.

Below A still from Sherlock Holmes' first appearance on film, the 30-second Sherlock Holmes Baffled *(1900).*

Bottom Gillette Castle, situated high above the Connecticut River, was built by actor William Gillette using the fortune he had earned playing Holmes on the stage.

which became the next main source for Holmes films.
Larsen directed and starred in *Arsène Lupin contre Sherlock
Holmes*, which ran to five episodes, made by the Berlin-
based Deutsche Vitaskop Company between 1910 and 1911.
These films seem to have been based on Maurice Leblanc's
similarly titled novels, which annoyed Conan Doyle, because
they appeared to him to be using the Sherlock Holmes name
contrary to existing copyright agreements.

They spurred Holmes's original creator to set aside
any concerns about the cinema (it seems copyright may have
been an issue) and sign a deal with the French
Éclair Company for a series of eight Anglo-French films
(all silent) made in Bexhill-on-Sea with British casts apart
from the Frenchman Georges Treville in the leading role.
Starting with *The Speckled Band*, released in November 1912,
these were at last faithful adaptations of the original stories.
But, despite his partial involvement, Conan Doyle doesn't
seem to have been well advised. He noted in *Memories
and Adventures*:

> Films of course were unknown when the stories
> appeared, and when these rights were finally
> discussed and a small sum offered for them by a
> French Company it seemed a treasure trove and
> I was very glad to accept. Afterwards I had to
> buy them back again at exactly ten times what
> I had received, so the deal was a disastrous one.

Another British film was made soon afterwards (in 1914)
by the Samuelson Company. This was *A Study in Scarlet*,
where Cheddar Gorge and Southport Sands in England
were required to stand in for the Rocky Mountains and
the plains of Utah. In 1916 Gillette himself made a film
version of his Sherlock Holmes play, directed by Arthur
Berthelet, for the Essanay Company, which had been
formed in Chicago nine years earlier. But by then, at the
age of over sixty, he was generally thought to be too old for
the part. More surprisingly, during the depths of the First
World War, Germany demonstrated its continuing love of
Holmes material with the release of *Der Hund von Baskerville*,
a passable version of the novel, made again by Deutsche
Vitaskop and starring Alwin Neuss.

Once the conflict was over Conan Doyle felt obliged to
explore the possibilities of an official Holmes film again. He
turned to the British Stoll Company, owned by the ambitious
impresario Sir Oswald Stoll. Having built up a chain of
theatres and music halls, including the London Coliseum,

in partnership with his mother, Stoll had recently turned to the cinema. He, or his powerful managing director Jeffrey Bernerd, surprised outsiders by picking another elderly actor Eille Norwood, who was almost sixty, to play Holmes. But Norwood was a pro who knew what he was doing. He wrote:

> My idea of Holmes is that he is absolutely quiet. Nothing ruffles him but he is a man who intuitively seizes points without revealing that he has done so and nurses them up with complete inaction until the moment when he is called upon to exercise his wonderful detective powers. He is like a cat – the person he is after is the only person in all the world, and he is oblivious of everything else till his quarry is run to earth.

As his deal with Stoll in March 1920 gave him 10 per cent of the overall receipts, Conan Doyle was openly appreciative, declaring of Norwood, 'He has that rare quality which can only be described as glamour, which compels you to watch an actor eagerly even when he is doing nothing. He has the brooding eye which excites expectation and he has also

a quite unrivalled power of disguise.' Norwood also was amazingly prolific: by April 1921 he had appeared in fifteen shortish films, starting with *The Dying Detective*, followed by another fifteen-part series (*The Adventures of Sherlock Holmes*) which was released from March 1922, and a further fifteen episodes (*The Last Adventures of Sherlock Holmes*) from March 1923. These films made no attempt to convey a period feel; they were unashamedly up-to-date, leading Conan Doyle to say his only complaint was that they introduced 'telephones, motor cars and other luxuries of which the Victorian Holmes never dreamed'.

Conan Doyle lent his support to the venture, appearing in person at the Stoll Film Convention, a big showcase for the company's productions, at the Trocadero restaurant in Shaftesbury Avenue in September 1921. The Holmes story, 'The Mazarin Stone', had just appeared in *The Strand Magazine*, a hasty adaptation from Conan Doyle's one-off play, *The Crown Diamond*, which had premièred earlier in the year. The Stoll gathering heard a message from the Prime Minister Lloyd George who claimed he had read this latest story and considered it one of the very best. Conan Doyle himself recalled his delight at learning of a party of French school children who, on being asked

Right Actor Eille Norwood appeared as Sherlock Holmes in nearly fifty films between 1921 and 1923.

Opposite A poster for Maurice Elvey's The Sign of Four *(1923) starring Eille Norwood.*

which one place in London they wanted to visit, replied 'Baker Street' (because they had been introduced to the great detective's adventures and thought it epitomized the British capital).

Having been a camera buff since his student days, Conan Doyle remained interested in photography of any kind. Now moving images were improving in quality, he saw their potential as a source of revenue for a writer. When asked by the novelist Mrs Humphrey Ward for advice in 1913 on how to approach this new-fangled phenomenon, he counselled her not to rush:

> for our rights are an asset which is rising in value, no one knows quite how much. English cinema films are in their infancy, but promise well, and it is there that our hopes lie. Unhappily the higher literature of thought and pathos is handicapped as compared to mere plot and action.

He seemed to be raising concerns that the screen might prove superior to the written word in conveying excitement rather than reflection.

After the First World War his own enthusiasm for photography took an unusual turn. Having dabbled with spiritualism for some years, he had finally embraced it wholeheartedly at the start of the war. He was now fascinated with the idea that it was possible to photograph spirit forms. What might have been a niche hobby became national news when, in 1920, he endorsed the claims of two Yorkshire girls to have photographed fairies (the famous Cottingley Fairies) in their back garden. A couple of years later he wrote a book titled *The Case for Spirit Photography*.

The new-found obsession took an unlikely turn when that same year, on a visit to the United States, he accepted an invitation from his friend Harry Houdini to address the annual banquet of the Society of American Magicians. The two men had been sparring about their different approaches to tricks: Conan Doyle thought Houdini's escapes required supernatural intervention, while the latter believed any so-called paranormal activity at séances and the like was fraudulent and could be explained rationally. At this event Conan Doyle surprised his audience by showing a short film which depicted lifelike dinosaurs in what seemed to be a prehistoric swamp. The attendees were dumbfounded by this apparent piece of magic in keeping with the traditions of their profession. It was only later that they learnt that Conan Doyle was showing them rushes from the film of his

book, *The Lost World*, and the dinosaurs' movements were achieved by an early use of the stop-motion or frame-to-frame animation technique (Willis O'Brien, one of the special-effects crew on *The Lost World*, would refine this technique in the movie *King Kong* a decade later).

With the Eille Norwood films continuing to roll out, 1922 also saw the release of *Sherlock Holmes*, another film version of the Gillette play, which came from the Goldwyn Studio in Hollywood. Over the previous decade this west-coast suburb of Los Angeles had established itself as the centre for the American movie industry. However, the eponymous Samuel Goldwyn was in the process of being removed by his partner and leading investor from control of the studio, and the remnant only soldiered on for a couple of years before being absorbed into MGM.

As the scion of a well-known theatrical family, the handsome, brooding actor John Barrymore brought star quality to the role of Holmes in the Goldwyn movie. The effects of his extravagant hard-drinking lifestyle added credence to his portrayal of the drug-taking detective. However, the critical consensus was that, despite fine location work in London and Switzerland, the film was unnecessarily slow. It was notable for the part of Professor

Moriarty which was played with great menace by the German Gustav von Seyffertitz.

However, the film led to a bitter copyright battle between the litigious Goldwyn Studio and Stoll, which had production facilities in Cricklewood in North London. The American company claimed it owned the rights to the Sherlock Holmes name, having bought them as part of its acquisition of Gillette's play. It was supported by both Gillette and Daniel Frohman, brother of Charles, who had backed the original production and later drowned in the sinking of the *Lusitania*. When the case reached the New York State Supreme Court in November 1920, it was rejected. But the plaintiffs appealed, forcing Conan Doyle to make a deposition which claimed that the Gillette play was a composite of several Holmes stories whereas the Stoll productions were based on specific stories. Again, the court found against Stoll and its allies.

Opposite Harry Houdini and Arthur Conan Doyle shake hands before Doyle departs for the UK after his visit to the United States in June 1922.

Below The Metro-Goldwyn-Mayer Studios in Culver City, California, in 1925.

But the proceedings had sullied the relationship between the author and Gillette, the man who had done so much to bring Sherlock Holmes to the general public. As a result of this legal fracas, and perhaps in tribute to von Seyffertitz's marvellous performance, the Barrymore film *Sherlock Holmes* had to be given the title *Moriarty* in the United Kingdom.

Conan Doyle was relieved when the film business took another turn and in 1929 the first Holmes talking picture ('talkie') was produced. This was *The Return of Sherlock Holmes*, based on the stories 'The Dying Detective' and *His Last Bow*. Directed by Basil Dean and produced by Paramount, a New York based production company headed by David Selznick, this film starred Clive Brook. Brook was another 'silent but sexy' British actor, who was under contract to Paramount where he had enjoyed recent success in *The Four Feathers*, one of the last films of the silent era. (Both silent and talking versions of *The Return of Sherlock Holmes* were made to accommodate theatres yet to make the transition.)

The 1930s would prove a golden age for the history of Sherlock Holmes on screen, giving rise to two great portrayals of the detective – by Arthur Wontner and Basil Rathbone. Wontner came to the role in 1931 when he appeared in *The Sleeping Cardinal*, a portmanteau title for a film which claimed to be based on the stories 'The Final Problem' and 'The Empty House' but which actually ploughed its own course through what *The Times* called 'a potpourri of all known social and domestic crimes', including a bank robbery and a villain called Robert Moriarty who wears dark glasses. This willingness to extend the range of the films outside the strict confines of the accepted canon followed the death of Conan Doyle himself in July 1930, after which management of his estate passed into the hands of his widow, Jean, and later his sons, Denis and Adrian.

With his chiselled features, gentlemanly manner and professional skill, Wontner is still regarded as one of the most canonically true exponents of Holmes on film. Vincent Starrett, the Sherlockian scholar, declared:

> … no better Sherlock Holmes than Arthur Wontner is likely to be seen and heard in pictures in our time. … His detective is the veritable fathomer of Baker Street in person. The keen worn, kindly face and quite prescient smile are out of the very pages of the book.

Right Poster for the silent 1922 drama Sherlock Holmes, *starring John Barrymore as Holmes, Roland Young as Watson and Gustav von Seyffertitz as Moriarty.*

Opposite In 1929, Basil Dean directed The Return of Sherlock Holmes, *the first sound film to feature Sherlock Holmes, starring Clive Brook.*

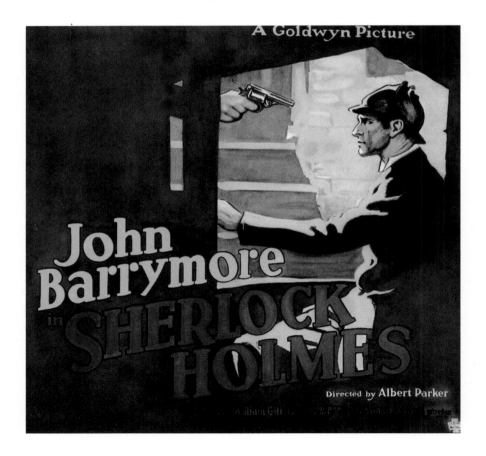

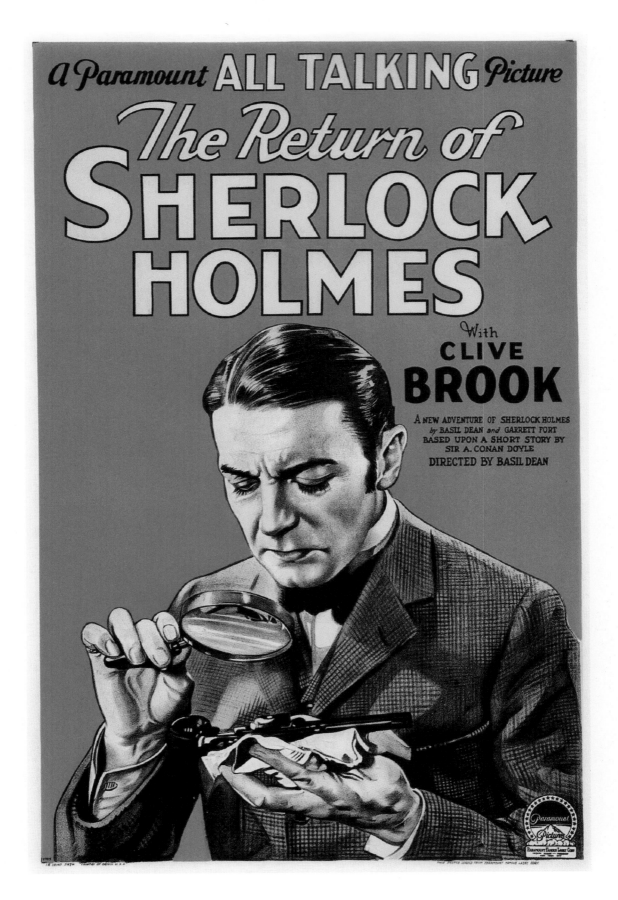

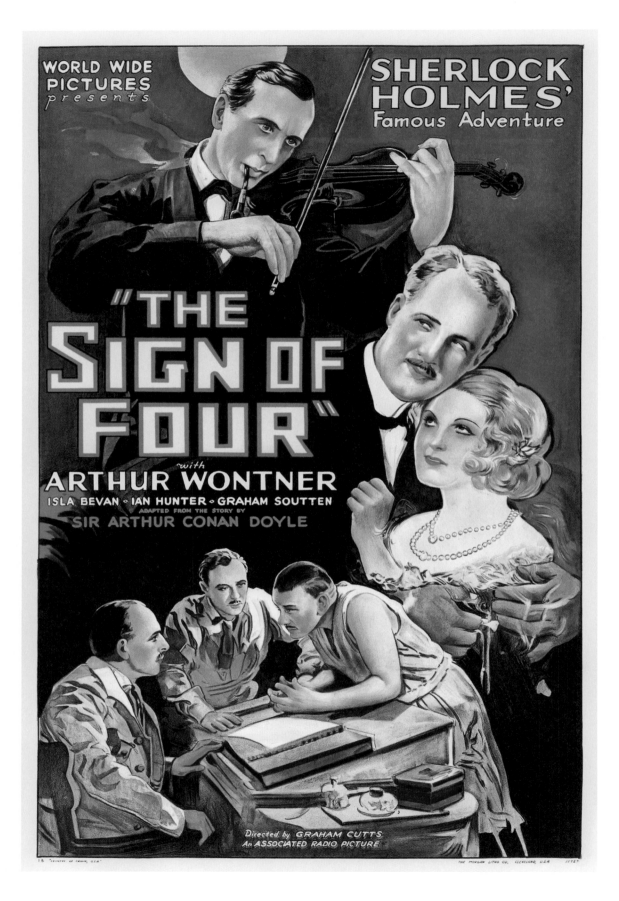

Wontner had experience playing sleuths on stage, notably Sax Rohmer's Paul Harley and Sexton Blake, perhaps the most direct cultural rival to Holmes at the time – a product of often garishly illustrated magazines and books by multiple authorial hands. He appeared as Holmes in four more films, including *The Triumph of Sherlock Holmes* (1935) where his Dr Watson was played by Ian Fleming, an established actor who was definitely not the creator of James Bond.

In 1937 Sherlock Holmes provided the content for an early drama broadcast by NBC through the new medium of television. At the time few people owned television sets, even in the United States, where they only entered mass production by RCA two years later, costing $445 at a time when the average American wage was $35 a month. The NBC show featured 'The Three Garridebs' and starred Louis Hector who had played Holmes in some of the episodes of a long-running radio series of Holmes stories which had aired between 1930 and 1936. The first of these radio programmes, which were broadcast live and so do not survive, starred the seventy-seven-year-old William Gillette.

The other great full-screen Holmes of the 1930s was Basil Rathbone, the South African-born son of a mining engineer, who appeared in *The Hound of the Baskervilles* and then *The Adventures of Sherlock Holmes* in 1939. He was the personal choice of Darryl F. Zanuck (the powerful head of the Twentieth Century Fox studio) for the role, which he reprised a further fourteen times. Full-screen was now the operative phrase; Holmes films had lately become B-movie material. With the imminent arrival of television in everyone's homes, it was therefore decided to compete by pitching Twentieth Century Fox's new series as big budget features. Recent productions had included contemporary backdrops, but Zanuck's studio invested in lavish sets which conveyed the true late nineteenth-century atmosphere of the original stories.

Best known of Rathbone's output was *The Hounds of the Baskervilles*. Though shot entirely on set in Hollywood, it vividly recreated the misty menace of Dartmoor and other period features. This excited the novelist Graham Greene who, in his capacity as a film critic for *The Spectator*, wrote:

In this new film Holmes is indubitably Holmes, and he hasn't to compete desperately with telephones and high speed cars and 1939. 'Your hat and boots, Watson, quick. Not a second to

lose!' He rushed into his room in his dressing gown and was back in a few seconds in a frock coat. The atmosphere of unmechanical Edwardian flurry is well caught: the villain bowls recklessly along Baker Street in a hansom and our hero discusses plans for action in a four-wheeler.

Rathbone was ably supported by Nigel Bruce, who played Dr Watson as Holmes's bumbling sidekick. Simultaneously, these two actors reprised the same roles in a new radio series, *The New Adventures of Sherlock Holmes*, which was masterminded by the ambitious Vassar-educated actor Edith Meiser and aimed to capitalize on the new much-publicized Twentieth Century Fox films. *The New Adventures of Sherlock Holmes* ran for 375 episodes from 1939 to 1950, more than half of them with Rathbone in the title role. A later British radio series, starring Carleton Hobbs, was a mere straggler in terms of longevity as it ran through seventy-five episodes of the Holmes stories on the BBC from 1952 to 1970 (initially as part of children's programming).

Unfortunately, Twentieth Century Fox's ambition was undermined by the grim realities of the Second World War in which Zanuck played a prominent operational role. After just two films the rights were transferred to Universal Studios which repackaged the stories as inferior propaganda vehicles. With names like *Sherlock Holmes in Washington* and *Sherlock Holmes Faces Death*, these movies saw the detective seeking out Nazi subversives, in a manner (albeit often entertaining) which was designed largely to promote the Allied wartime cause, but which were a long way from Conan Doyle's originals. After a while the producers even gave up using the name Sherlock Holmes in the titles, so Rathbone and Bruce starred in further films such as *Spider Woman* (1944) and *Pursuit to Algiers* (1945). Well before these ended, Rathbone was resenting being typecast, so he didn't mind when the series drew to an end with *Dressed to Kill* in 1946.

It seemed the viewing public had had enough of Conan Doyle's consulting detective for the time being, because he didn't reappear on celluloid until 1959 when the British company Hammer Films produced *The Hound of the*

Opposite Basil Rathbone in The Hound of the Baskervilles *(1939).*

Below A poster for Hammer's horror version of The Hound of the Baskervilles *(1959) starring Peter Cushing.*

Baskervilles, the first Sherlock Holmes film shot in colour. Hammer had made its name earlier in the decade with its gaudy sensationalist horror films, notably *Dracula*. It transferred two of the stars of that movie to *The Hound of the Baskervilles*, casting Peter Cushing as Holmes and Christopher Lee as Sir Henry Baskerville. (Lee had played Dracula in the earlier film, Cushing the scientist Professor van Helsing.) The team brought a horror film energy and pizzazz to *The Hound of the Baskervilles*, much of which was actually filmed on Dartmoor. Despite the film's success (it was released in the United States by Universal), Hammer was unable to reach terms with the Conan Doyle Estate and did not make another Holmes film. Cushing was more lucky, playing the detective in the second series of a new BBC television adaptation of the canon in 1968. Meanwhile Lee had an unusual outing as Holmes in a 1962 German film *Sherlock Holmes und Das Halsband des Todes* (*Sherlock Holmes and the Necklace of Death*) – a project which did have the estate's imprimatur, but which left even Lee himself unimpressed, describing it as 'a badly edited, deplorable hodge podge of nonsense'.

Cerebral by nature and generally sexless by choice, Holmes now had to deal with a major change in society.

Sexual intercourse was famously (but erroneously) said by Philip Larkin to have begun in 1963. The previous year had seen the first James Bond film *Dr No*, and, in the cinema world, that changed everything. The vogue was now for sexually explicit action-packed movies that tried to keep up with 007's exploits. Unable to compete on these terms, Holmes film producers initially dialled up the violence. *A Study in Terror*, shot at Shepperton and released in 1965 by Hammer Films with the Conan Doyle Estate (through Sir Nigel Films) as a co-producer, was the first X-rated Holmes film. It pitched Holmes into the rough and tumble of London's East End trying to solve the Jack the Ripper murders. He was played with commendable vigour by John Neville, who – like several before him – had learned his craft playing Shakespeare. He had one particular advantage in that he was youthful. But, despite Judi Dench (later 'M' in the Bond movies) appearing in a small part, Hammer's effort flopped and the estate's plans for further films from the same stable were shelved. *A Study in Terror* was generally panned, though *Time* magazine did have some good words for it, describing it as 'sly and stylish' and adding, 'Bonds may come and Maigrets may go, but Sherlock Holmes goes on forever'.

Right Christopher Lee and Thorley Walters in Sherlock Holmes und Das Halsband des Todes *(1962).*

Opposite A poster for A Study in Terror *(1965), starring John Neville.*

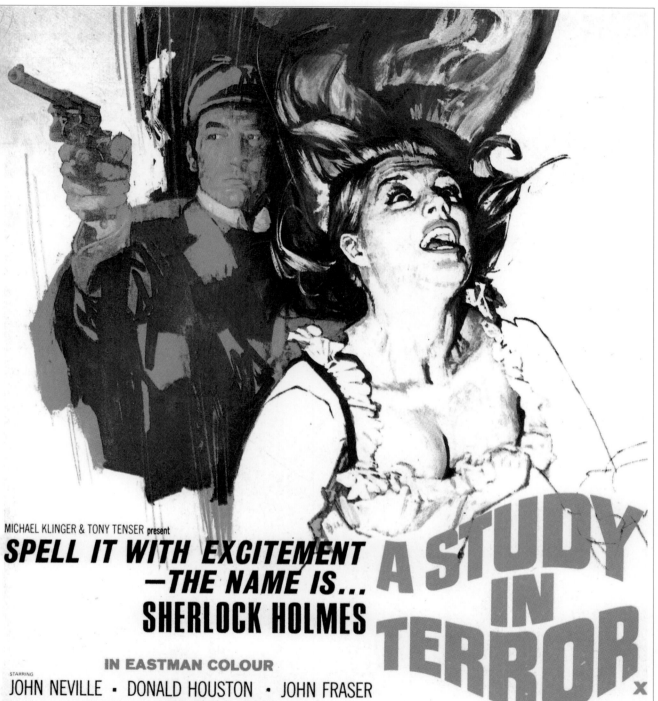

MICHAEL KLINGER & TONY TENSER present

SPELL IT WITH EXCITEMENT —THE NAME IS... SHERLOCK HOLMES

A STUDY IN TERROR

x

IN EASTMAN COLOUR

STARRING

JOHN NEVILLE · DONALD HOUSTON · JOHN FRASER
ANTHONY QUAYLE · BARBARA WINDSOR

SPECIAL GUEST STAR

ROBERT MORLEY ·

GUEST STARS

GEORGIA BROWN · BARRY JONES · CECIL PARKER

EXECUTIVE PRODUCER

HERMAN COHEN ·

PRODUCED BY

HENRY E. LESTER ·

DIRECTED BY

JAMES HILL · A COMPTON-SIR NIGEL FILMS PRODUCTION

The more liberal atmosphere of the 1970s had other repercussions. It was now acceptable to be irreverent about Sherlock Holmes – a factor which proved a blessing in disguise, as it helped two left-field productions revive Holmes's fortunes by showing that he could be presented creatively in different ways. One, in 1970, was *The Private Life of Sherlock Holmes* which, as Watson stated at the start, purported to recount those adventures of the detective 'which, for reason for discretion, I have decided to withhold from the public until this much later date'. Briskly directed and lovingly produced by Billy Wilder at Pinewood, the film showed Holmes, played by the accomplished Robert Stephens, taking cocaine, cavorting with a prostitute and indulging in an affair with a glamorous Belgian woman, while apparently also protesting his firm affection for Watson. A long-gestated romantic extravaganza as conceived by Wilder, it had to be drastically cut to meet the demands of Universal Pictures. The other new cinematic departure, in 1975, was *The Adventure of Sherlock Holmes' Smarter Brother*, directed by the American comic actor Gene Wilder (no relation) and starring Douglas Wilmer, who had played Holmes in the first series of the BBC television adaptation a decade earlier (before giving way

to Peter Cushing). Neither film was popular commercially, though both have retrospectively grown in stature. By then Holmes had recovered some artistic credibility, following an unlikely but successful restaging of Gillette's original play *Sherlock Holmes* by Britain's Royal Shakespeare Company at the Aldwych Theatre and the publication of Nicholas Meyer's novel *The Seven-Per-Cent Solution*, an iconoclastic romp in which Holmes visits Sigmund Freud in Vienna to cure his opium addiction. The book was promptly transferred to the screen with another revered British thespian Nicol Williamson in the lead as Holmes.

Two films with established British stars failed to make the cut. Given the parallels with James Bond, Roger Moore was just too smooth to play Holmes in *Sherlock Holmes in New York*, a TV movie produced by Twentieth Century Fox

Opposite Holmes meets Freud in The Seven-Per-Cent Solution *(1976) starring Nicol Williamson and Alan Arkin.*

Below A still from The Private Life of Sherlock Holmes *(1970).*

in 1976. (By then he had already appeared in two 007 films, starting with *Live and Let Die* in 1973.) And John Cleese wasn't aiming for immortality when he reprised the role for laughs in *Elementary My Dear Watson* (1973) and in the clearly uncanonical *The Strange Case of the End of Civilisation As We Know It* (1977). Peter Cook was another comic who wrongly saw Sherlock Holmes as a vehicle for his talents, starring in a self-styled parody *The Hound of the Baskervilles* (1977), with his revue partner Dudley Moore as Dr Watson. ('It's a real howl!' ran one of the promotional posters.)

By now other forces were at work in the film industry. The old studios no longer held sway in Hollywood, and the economics of movie-making had changed. Already it was clear from films such as *The Private Life of Sherlock Holmes* that there was room for alternative, sometimes disrespectful, approaches to depicting the detective's adventures.

Searching for the magic formula, some film and TV executives thought that Holmes might benefit from being targeted at a younger audience. Granada's Michael Cox offered *Young Sherlock: The Mystery of the Manor House*, an eight-part television series that ran in 1982, starring Guy Henry as a seventeen-year-old Sherlock. Amongst other feats, the young Sherlock unravelled a conspiracy against

Queen Victoria. Three years later a more ambitious feature film arrived with a very similar title, *Young Sherlock Holmes*, with Nicholas Rowe as Holmes and Alan Cox as Watson meeting at school and thwarting a dastardly plot by an ancient Egyptian cult of Osiris worshippers. With Steven Spielberg as one of the producers, this film took Sherlock Holmes films into new territory with its innovative use of digital imaging: indeed, it was the first feature film to include a completely computer-generated character. In another tilt at a younger demographic, in 1986 Walt Disney came up with an animated film, *The Great Mouse Detective*, based on Basil of Baker Street, a series of books centred on a sleuth living in Holmestead, a community of mice in the basement of 221B Baker Street.

These developments were played out against a complex backdrop of the Holmes stories themselves beginning to fall out of copyright and into the public domain. This coincided with a period when the Conan Doyle Estate was in disarray. Stewardship of this valuable cultural property had passed to Conan Doyle's two sons, Denis and Adrian, who frittered away the accruing financial assets. For a while a rival estate owned some of the copyrights, leading to confusion among filmmakers. Eventually, following

Opposite Roger Moore, with Charlotte Rampling and Patrick Macnee, in Sherlock Holmes in New York *(1976).*

Left Dudley Moore, Kenneth Williams and Peter Cook in The Hound of the Baskervilles *(1977).*

Below Alan Cox and Nicholas Rowe in Young Sherlock Holmes *(1985).*

the early deaths of her brothers, Conan Doyle's surviving daughter, Jean, was able to wrest back control. She was helped by changes in the US and EU law which extended the length of copyright in books and films to up to seventy-five years after they were created.

A return to relative stability came with the success of Holmes's latest manifestation on television – the Granada series *Sherlock Holmes*, which ran over forty-one critically acclaimed and canonically faithful episodes from 1984 to 1994. Jeremy Brett, as the detective, was happy to explore his character's personality weaknesses in a way that had not been really tried before. So the series presented Holmes as a neurotic obsessive, eager to resort to his favourite narcotics. It helped that Brett himself was a troubled character, subject to wild mood swings and breakdowns.

Then, towards the end of the first decade of the twenty-first century, a new round of interest in Sherlock Holmes emerged, as the different mediums of film and television

competed to bring both the characters and the cultural context up to date with the internet age. Convinced that the Holmes stories contained all the necessary excitement and action to compete in this new environment, Lionel Wigram, a senior vice-president at Warner Brothers, teamed up with the British director Guy Ritchie to produce a turbo-charged version of the Holmes story, with the main character a fast-talking bare-knuckle fighter and martial-arts enthusiast. Together they prevailed on the major Hollywood actor Robert Downey Jr. to take the leading role, with Jude Law as Dr Watson and a strong female interest in Rachael McAdams as Irene Adler. Released in 2009, the film simply called *Sherlock Holmes* was a huge hit, netting over half a billion dollars in box office receipts and winning several awards. It quickly spawned a sequel, *Sherlock Holmes: A Game of Shadows* (2011) which was a similar commercial success. However, a rumoured third film failed to appear, and the talk in 2023, a dozen years later, was of plans for a television 'universe', similar to that created by Marvel Comics, which would allow several spin-offs to be made.

At much the same time Steven Moffat and Mark Gatiss, multi-talented writers and directors who had worked together on *Dr Who*, dreamed up a new television

Opposite Jeremy Brett appeared in forty-one episodes of Granada TV's Sherlock Holmes *series between 1984 and 1994.*

Below Robert Downey Jr. in Guy Ritchie's action-packed Sherlock Holmes *(2009).*

Above Benedict Cumberbatch as the consulting detective in Mark Gatiss's and Steven Moffat's modern-day Sherlock *(2010–17).*

Right 'Holmes' became 'House' in the eponymous US medical drama starring Hugh Laurie, which ran for eight seasons between 2004 and 2012.

Opposite American crime drama Elementary *(2012–19) starred Jonny Lee Miller as Sherlock Holmes and Lucy Liu as Dr Joan Watson.*

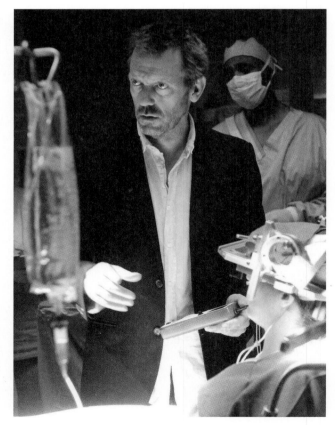

series based in contemporary London which would show Holmes solving a series of mysteries, borrowing from rather than relying religiously on the Conan Doyle stories. As a novel development, their Holmes would use modern telecommunications technology, particularly mobile phones and the internet, to negotiate his urban environment and solve his mysteries. Having seen Benedict Cumberbatch, one of the best young actors in Britain, in the film *Atonement*, their production company, Hartsmoor, chose him to play Holmes, with Martin Freeman as Dr Watson. Hartsmoor sold the idea to the BBC in Britain and to PBS in the United States. An initial pilot episode won few plaudits and only appeared later on DVD, but four three-part series, comprising 85–90-minute films, were aired under the rubric *Sherlock* between 2010 and 2017 and proved extraordinarily popular throughout the world, selling to 180 countries.

Similar initiatives came with *House*, a television series clearly inspired by Holmes, which ran on Fox in the United States for eight seasons and 176 episodes from 2004 to 2012; it featured a drug-addicted doctor, played by Hugh Laurie, living at Apartment B, 221 Baker Street. Another successful television series with the same antecedents was *Elementary*, starring Jonny Lee Miller, which translated Holmes, a

recovering drug addict, from London to New York where, with a female assistant, Dr Joan Watson (played by Lucy Liu) he helps the Police Department with a variety of cases presented in police procedural style (running to an astonishing 154 episodes). On the cinema screen, *Mr Holmes*, a 2015 film with Ian McKellan in the lead, took a different approach, drawing on Mitch Cullin's novel *A Slight Trick of the Mind* to show the detective in retirement as he tries to piece together an old case through the haze of memory loss.

One result of Sherlock's global success on the screen was that several similar series have appeared abroad. The eight-part *Sherlock: The Russian Chronicles* directed by Nurbek Egen transplanted Holmes to St Petersburg where he rediscovers his yen for chemistry and reads Dostoevsky. In Japan Fuji Television's *Sherlock: Untold Stories* followed the BBC's *Sherlock* in using contemporary locations, rapid scene changes and the latest technical gadgets, particularly relating to personal communications. Starring Dean Fujioka as the consulting detective Shishio Homare, this ran for twelve episodes in late 2019, with a feature-length film version – *The Hound of the Baskervilles: Sherlock the Movie* – in 2022.

Japan's enthusiasm for Sherlock Holmes led to the commissioning there of *Miss Sherlock*, which for the first time cast not only Holmes (played by Yuko Takeuchi) but also Watson (Shihori Kanjiya) as women. After successful airings in Japan and across Asia, this quirky show was taken up by Hulu and HBO, the original producers, for US audiences in 2018. It was followed two years later by the Netflix presentation of *Enola Holmes* starring Millie Bobby Brown as Holmes's teenage sister, determined to follow in his footsteps. This proved so popular that a second film titled unimaginatively *Enola Holmes 2* followed in 2022.

By then the renewed worldwide fascination with the detective had brought the story back full circle to Gillette, as it encouraged a revival in stage versions of the stories, often presented in theatres outside the West End or Broadway. This process began slowly when the play *The Secret of Sherlock Holmes*, originally a vehicle for Jeremy Brett in the late 1980s, was taken up and given a new lease of life by Peter Egan, who toured the provinces of Britain with it in 2010. This ran in parallel with the canonically inspired output of actors such as Roger Llewellyn who led the way in presenting productions in small spaces with pared-down casts, often comprising just

Holmes and Watson. And these grassroot developments were replicated throughout the world. A Christmas offering in Canada in 2022 was *Holmes for the Holidays*, the self-described story of 'Broadway star' William Gillette, who invites members of his cast back to his castle for a weekend of revelry. 'But the festivities in this isolated house of tricks and mirrors quickly turn dangerous when a guest is killed!' Clearly the theatrical and cinematic possibilities of the Holmes stories never cease.

Below Yuko Takeuchi and Shihori Kanjiya as Holmes and Watson in HBO Asia's Miss Sherlock *(2018).*

GETTING INTO PRINT

Would we still be reading Sherlock Holmes if his exploits had not been packaged into a series which ran in a new publication called *The Strand Magazine* from July 1891? It's like asking if James Bond would still be remembered if he hadn't been portrayed on the cinema screen by Sean Connery in 1962. Holmes had already appeared in a couple of short books – *A Study in Scarlet* and *The Sign of Four* – by mid-1891. He had been well received, his character as a reclusive sleuth living somewhat eccentrically in Baker Street had been nicely delineated, but he had hardly set the world on fire. It was only after he had been portrayed in the new mass-market monthly, *The Strand Magazine*, along with appropriate illustrations by Sidney Paget, that he really took off. And that would not have happened without the convergence of other factors in the literary, publishing and wider worlds.

The immediate story goes back a decade to 24 August 1881, more or less exactly when Dr Watson was first meeting Sherlock Holmes. On that day thirty-year-old George Newnes, a restless assistant in a haberdashery shop in Manchester, read a short item entitled 'A Runaway Train' in a local newspaper. This gave him the idea of setting up a magazine devoted to similar arresting snippets,

or tit-bits, of news. Within weeks, on 22 October, he published the first issue of *Tit-Bits*, or, to give it its full title, *Tit-Bits from all the Interesting Books, Periodicals, and Newspapers of the World*. With additional ingredients such as competitions, puzzles and give-aways, this weekly Google-type trawl of existing printed media cost a penny an issue. It was an immediate success, allowing it to move its headquarters to 12 Burleigh Street, on the corner of the Strand in London's West End, in 1884.

By the end of the decade *Tit-Bits* had spawned a couple of equally successful competitors. One of these rivals was *Answers to Correspondents*, which offered a similar formula of short, sharp items of news and information, as gathered by Alfred Harmsworth, the young editor of *Cycling News*. The other was *Pearson's Weekly*, founded by Arthur Pearson, who had worked for Newnes at *Tit-Bits*.

By January 1890 Newnes was earning £30,000 a year (or £4.5 million today) and looking to expand his publishing empire. He teamed up with a like-minded journalist, W.T. Stead, to produce a slightly more up-market periodical, the *Review of Reviews*. But the two men quickly fell out over Stead's muck-raking tendencies (*Tit-Bits*, for all its potentially titillating name, adopted a

high moral tone). The sticking point was Stead's insistence on publishing Leo Tolstoy's *The Kreutzer Sonata*, a radical attack on marriage which had been banned in the author's native Russia.

So Newnes adapted the model for *The Strand Magazine*, the first issue of which was published in January 1891. This was a monthly magazine, comprising stories and articles, costing sixpence (roughly half the price of competitors), and aimed at a family market – particularly the sort of office worker who might buy a copy to read on a train and bring it home for his wife and children to read at the weekend. The initial issue sold out and *The Strand Magazine* was soon selling 300,000 copies a month.

An essential feature was the new periodical's profuse use of illustrations. British magazines felt vulnerable to American competitors, which were livelier and cheaper (as a result of using the new half-tone process of photographic reproduction). Having invested in similar competitive machines (notably a US-made rotary art press, which could print sixty-four illustrated pages with one rotation of a drum), Newnes was determined to take full advantage of the opportunities this gave, and this meant allowing as much illustration as possible.

Around this time, Conan Doyle was beginning his literary career. A bit earlier, after contributing stories (often involving the paranormal) to established review-style periodicals such as *The Cornhill* and *Belgravia: A London Magazine* and feeling he wasn't getting anywhere, he decided he wanted his name on the 'back of a volume'. Having recently got married, he decided, as a sideline to his main profession as a doctor, to write a detective story featuring Sherlock Holmes. It turned out to be a novella of just over 43,000 words – short enough for serialization, but also publishable in book form as he wanted. He tried it on his friend James Payn, editor of *The Cornhill*, but Payn thought its 'penny dreadful' style inappropriate for his magazine. So, the story took a 'circular tour' of some second-division book publishers, earning rejections from Arrowsmith's and Frederick Warne, before finding a berth at Ward Lock, which offered Conan Doyle a paltry £25 for all rights. *A Study in Scarlet* was published in Ward Lock's popular *Beeton's Christmas Annual* in November 1887 and finally achieved its author's ambition of appearing in book form under that publisher's imprint the following year.

This title and its successor, *The Sign of Four* (published by the American *Lippincott's Monthly Magazine* in February 1890

Opposite Beeton's Christmas Annual *1887 featured* A Study in Scarlet, *the very first appearance of Sherlock Holmes.*

Left This Edwardian postcard *features a fish delivery boy distracted by* Tit-Bits *magazine.*

and in hardback by Spencer Blackett later that year), enjoyed some critical success, but no great sales. However, they had brought Conan Doyle to the notice of a circle of writers centred on London's Savile Club. There he had met the author Walter Besant who, at his request, had recommended a literary agent, A.P. (Alexander) Watt, who also had the rising star Rudyard Kipling on his books. Agents at the time were a new and not always welcome feature of the publishing ecosystem. But Besant was a great champion of the writing profession (he had founded the Society of Authors in 1884). Having taken his advice, Conan Doyle was able to move to London and commit himself more fully to the business of writing (initially in tandem with medicine).

His first letter to his new agent in September 1890 dealt with his novel *The White Company*. But the astute Watt had taken note of *The Strand Magazine*'s arrival three months later and immediately identified it as an outlet for his new client. Conan Doyle was still in Vienna when his first piece for *The Strand Magazine*, 'The Voice of Science', was published in March 1891. This was a light-hearted satire about the aspirations of a provincial scientific-cum-literary society, which was about as far from a detective story as could be imagined. Yet he had impressed the periodical's editor,

Herbert Greenhough Smith, for when, at the end of that month, Watt sent him Conan Doyle's 8,600-word story 'A Scandal in Bohemia', featuring his fictional sleuth, Sherlock Holmes, he immediately accepted it, offering Conan Doyle four pounds per thousand words, a healthy premium on his usual fee. (Greenhough Smith was officially the Literary Editor because the title of editor was reserved for Newnes, but Greenhough Smith took the decisions on the contents.)

Somewhere down the line the decision was made that Holmes and his companion Dr Watson would feature in a series of stand-alone stories (rather than the old-fashioned serial, which required a cliff-hanger at the end of each episode). So, *The Strand Magazine*'s art editor, W.H.J. Boot was able to order a run of distinctive drawings from Sidney Paget. (The story, never fully substantiated, was that Boot intended to commission Sidney's brother, Walter, who, like him, had attended the Royal Academy Schools. But somehow the letter reached the wrong person, and Sidney got the job that made his name.) Paget's characterization of Holmes as inquisitive, lithe and angular in appearance established the detective's image in perpetuity. It was well served by the halftone photomechanical engraving process, which enabled Paget's fluid brushwork to be

Right Sidney Paget, the main illustrator of the Holmes stories in The Strand Magazine.

Opposite Sherlock Holmes and Twelve Scenes from His Career, *a composite image incorporating material from several artists, mainly Sidney Paget, used as frontispiece to 'The Red Circle',* The Strand Magazine, *March 1908.*

turned into plates from which the printed page was made. In all, ten Paget drawings were used over the fourteen pages in *The Strand Magazine* devoted to the publication of 'A Scandal in Bohemia'.

A feature of the magazine was its pale green-blue cover designed by George Charles Haité, which showed the bustling thoroughfare known as Strand from the corner of Burleigh Street, where its offices were originally situated.

The magazine could not have existed without an eager readership. This had been considerably boosted by the steady advance of universal education which followed Forster's Elementary Education Act of 1870. This piece of legislation was introduced to ensure that the million or so male property owners who had been enfranchised by the Second Reform Act of 1867 had at least some level of basic learning. As a result, local authorities were compelled to provide schooling for children between the ages of five and twelve, and, if there was no provision, they had to establish their own 'board schools' – of the type which Sherlock Holmes enthusiastically described to Watson in 'The Naval Treaty' as 'lighthouses, my boy! Beacons of the future! Capsules with hundreds of bright little seeds in each, out of which will spring the wiser, better England of the future.'

Below The Book Shop *(1899), lithograph, by Francis Donkin Bedford (1864–1954).*

Opposite The W.H. Smith *bookstall at Charing Cross station, London (c.1890).*

CHARING CROSS STATION

With modern production methods, the price of
magazines fell dramatically both to cater for and then as
a result of the demand from these new readers. Sixty years
earlier, a monthly magazine such as *Bentley's Miscellany*
cost two shillings and sixpence. Around the middle of the
century a similar publication such as *The Cornhill* sold for
one shilling. But *The Strand Magazine* could be bought for
sixpence ('a monthly magazine costing sixpence but worth
a shilling' was its advertising slogan), and it duly reaped
its reward in vastly increased sales.

The book trade was forced to follow suit. In the
1830s, novels had been published largely in three-volume
octavo editions costing half a guinea (ten shillings and
sixpence, or the equivalent of £50 at 2023 prices) a
volume. Such books, known as triple-deckers, were sold to
a restricted market through book clubs such as Mudie's.
Over the succeeding decades, rises in population and
disposable income created a wider readership which
gradually made inroads into this virtual monopoly.
Supportive developments included the Public Libraries
Act of 1850, which encouraged councils to set up free
libraries, increased discounting, and the success of
W.H. Smith's railway bookstalls, which led to a variety

of cheap editions such as George Routledge's shilling
Railway Library.

By the end of the century, the publishing business was
experiencing the same changes as magazines. Its provincial
structure (Arrowsmith's, which rejected *A Study in Scarlet*,
had been based in Bristol) was giving way to a more
metropolitan model, with companies such as Longman,
Macmillan and John Murray still leading the way, but with
new, now recognisable names such as Heinemann and
Edwin Arnold setting up in London in 1890, along with
Constable (a revival of an old Edinburgh firm).

While magazines are hardly mentioned in the
Sherlock Holmes stories, books are often referred to,
though usually unnamed. Smoking a last pipe at the end of
an exhausting day in 'The Adventure of the Crooked Man'
Watson finds himself nodding off over a novel. Having
newly arrived in Britain, Sir Henry Baskerville takes
stock of the situation in *The Hound of the Baskervilles* and
decides he has just 'walked into the thick of a dime novel'.
And there is an interesting self-mocking exchange in
The Valley of Fear when, while chatting to Inspector
Macdonald about Professor Moriarty, Holmes mentions
someone called Jonathan Wild. Macdonald immediately

READING OF THE PERIOD.

responds, 'Well, the name has a familiar sound. Someone in a novel, was he not? I don't take much stock of detectives in novels – chaps that do things and never let you see how they do them. That's just inspiration: not business.' Holmes replies, 'Jonathan Wild wasn't a detective, and he wasn't in a novel. He was a master criminal, and he lived last century – 1750 or thereabouts.' He tells Macdonald that he would benefit from three months' reading up on the history of English crime. 'Everything comes in circles,' says Holmes. 'Even Professor Moriarty. Jonathan Wild was the hidden force of the London criminals, to whom he sold his brains and his organization on a 15 per cent commission.'

Occasionally, as in 'The Adventure of the Copper Beeches', a novel is described as 'yellow-backed'. This refers to one of the cheaper types of novel which flourished in the 1870s and 1880s in new marketplaces such as W.H. Smith's railway bookstalls. There they competed with other forms of popular reading matter, including the original penny dreadfuls and dime novels. Penny dreadfuls (or, more explicitly, 'penny bloods') were uncompromisingly sensationalist literature, often with Gothic or pirate themes. They grew out of earlier true-crime broadsheets, using the same type of crudely drawn illustrations, printed on cheap wood-pulp paper, and crucially aimed at the emerging market of newly literate young working-class men, who could just about afford the penny price tag. Dime novels were more of an American phenomenon – cheaply produced adventure stories and romances. It's curious that they are even mentioned in the canon, but it is likely that their fare of Western and frontier themes was enjoyed by the young Conan Doyle.

Yellowbacks arrived when publishers upped their game to remain competitive and were still able to produce inexpensive hardback novels. They were generally small crown octavo in format, bound in thin strawboard cases, covered with coloured (usually yellow) paper which had been block printed with vivid pictures. This required a new technique called chromoxylography which, when

Opposite An engraving of young Victorian women reading advertisements for penny dreadful books, 1870.

Below The Parisian Novels (The Yellow Books) *(1887), oil on canvas, by Vincent van Gogh (1853–90).*

149

combined with expert engraving, allowed the mixing of several colour hues.

Yellowbacks are not to be confused with *The Yellow Book*, the influential magazine associated with the aesthetic movement of the 1890s. Published at the Bodley Head by Elkin Matthews and John Lane, *The Yellow Book* developed its Art Nouveau style partly from its first art director, Aubrey Beardsley. Although mentioned in *The Portrait of Dorian Gray*, it never featured the work of Oscar Wilde (or indeed of Conan Doyle), but was associated with figures such as Max Beerbohm.

The appearance of *The Yellow Book* reflected a chasm in English letters – something that Conan Doyle managed to negotiate in his inimitable way. In the last decade of the nineteenth century, fiction writing became polarized between realists and modernists. One camp looked back to the great tradition of British novelists, such as Dickens, and was generally opposed to incursions by females or foreigners. Its values were reflected in the group of writers known as the Henley Regatta who followed W.E. Henley, author of the popular poem 'Invictus' and editor of the *Scots* (later *National*) *Observer*, in promoting hearty masculine values in literature.

The other camp was more open to modernizing influences, such as symbolism, naturalism and even decadence, which tended to come from Europe and were evident in *The Yellow Book*.

Conan Doyle followed the Henley Regatta in admiring the traditional romance or adventure story associated with Robert Louis Stevenson. But he was open enough to appreciate the art of the Frenchman Émile Zola who, in *Le Roman Expérimental*, had proposed a more scientific focus to the novel, advocating, 'We must operate with characters, passions, human and social data as the chemist and physicist work on inert bodies, as the physiologist works on living bodies.' Conan Doyle's ability to combine the ideals of both camps played an important part in the success of Sherlock Holmes, who was both a romantic adventurer (in Stevenson terms) and an aesthete.

Right Portrait of Robert Louis Stevenson (1887), oil on canvas, by John Singer Sargent (1856–1925).

ART IN
THE BLOOD

For a man described by his closest companion as 'an automaton – a calculating machine', Sherlock Holmes certainly has a developed aesthetic sense. Music is his thing (he likes to scrape away at his violin and go to concerts), but, as the great-nephew of the celebrated French artist Émile Jean-Horace Vernet, he also knows his painting and sculpture. In that last respect at least, he is similar to his creator, who came from a family of notable artists. But Arthur Conan Doyle had little or no aptitude for music. He liked the theatre, but did not go to concerts or opera.

Both men (fictional and real) inhabited a period of transformation in the arts. Modernism had yet to surface, but the late nineteenth century, and particularly the 1890s – when these two characters – first flourished, nevertheless saw significant innovations in this field.

Some of this came from the very skill in which both Holmes and Conan Doyle excelled – simple observation. The process of looking at objects and representing them had taken a leap forward with the work of the British photographer Eadweard Muybridge who, in the late 1870s, used quick, multiple exposures of images to show how animals and human beings actually moved.

Looking at the world differently coincided with changes in chronology and narrative perspective in literature, as found in the work of novelists such as Fyodor Dostoevsky, Gustave Flaubert and Wilkie Collins. Already these subtle adjustments were being absorbed into the output of artists such as Edouard Manet and the Impressionists from the 1860s. Further developments, including Art Nouveau, Pointillism and Symbolism accelerated these moves. Paul Gauguin's *Manao Tupapau (The Spirit of the Dead Keeps Watch)*, shows symbolism being embraced, while not totally rejecting the existing traditions of art. (It was painted in 1892, the year that *The Adventures of Sherlock Holmes* first appeared in book form.) It wasn't long before the art world was completely turned upside down, with the arrival of Cubism (from Pablo Picasso and Georges Braque in 1907) and Futurism (from Filippo Tommaso Marinetti a couple of years later).

In this context, the tastes of both Holmes and Conan Doyle were conservative. The former took his pictorial cues from his artistic great-uncle Émile Jean-Horace (known as Horace) Vernet (1789–1863), whose father Carle Vernet (1758–1836) and grandfather Claude-Joseph Vernet (1714–89) were also well-known French painters. And even Claude-Joseph's father, Antoine, was described as an artisan painter, making four generations of that family artists and giving Holmes ample scope to gather the material for his observation in 'The Adventure of the Greek Interpreter' that 'art in the blood is liable to take the strangest forms'.

The Vernets' general artistic style as a family can be described as conventional. Claude-Joseph specialized in seascapes; Carle, known for his equestrian studies, became court painter to Louis XVIII; and Horace was famed for his detailed battle scenes, as well as his Orientalist subject matter. Horace also had royalist connections, having enjoyed the patronage of the Duke of Orléans, later King Louis-Philippe, who ruled France from 1830–48.

Considering that there's not much cultural experimentation in Holmes's background, it's odd to recall his quasi-Bohemian lifestyle. He 'loathed every form of society with his whole Bohemian soul', we are told in the appropriately named 'A Scandal in Bohemia'. Watson refers elsewhere ('The Adventure of the Engineer's Thumb') to his colleague's 'natural Bohemianism'. But it's a vague line of thought that is only found in the early stories – shortly after Conan Doyle himself was flirting with the *fin de siècle* world of Oscar Wilde, whose company he had enjoyed over dinner at the Langham Hotel in August 1889.

Holmes himself was better acquainted with music than with art. He relaxed at Baker Street by playing his violin. This was a Stradivarius, worth at least 500 guineas, which he had bought for 45 shillings in a pawnbroker's shop in London's Tottenham Court Road. He prided himself on his knowledge of his instruments, for Watson noted his companion's high spirits as he 'prattled away about Cremona fiddles and the difference between a Stradivarius and an Amati.'

Indeed, his general musical knowledge seems to have been good. In 'The Adventure of the Cardboard Box' Watson recalled him reminiscing about Paganini, 'and we sat for an hour over a bottle of claret while he told me anecdote after anecdote of that extraordinary man.'

As the author of a monograph on the 'Polyphonic Motets of Lassus', mentioned in 'The Adventure of the Bruce-Partington Plans', Holmes could even be described as scholarly. This was the sixteenth-century Flemish composer Orlande (or Roland) de Lassus (1532–94), now relatively forgotten, but in his day a rival to Palestrina in his output of religious music, Italian madrigals, French chansons and German lieder, including 516 motets, which were choral works of interactive voices sung in Latin. Sticklers have queried why this monograph should refer tautologically to

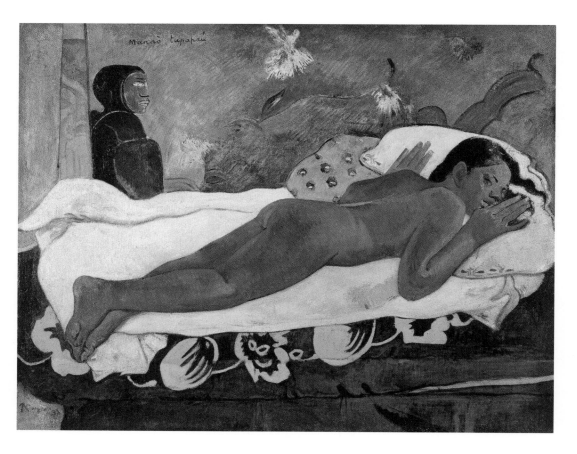

Opposite Manao Tupapau (The Spirit of the Dead Watches) *(1892), oil on canvas, by Paul Gauguin (1848–1903).*

Above The Battle of Valmy, 20 September 1792 *(1826), oil on canvas, by Horace Vernet (1789–1863).*

Left Portrait of the Flemish composer Orlande de Lassus, *about whose motets Holmes wrote a scholarly monograph.*

Above Holmes's favourite
violinist, Wilma Norman-Neruda
(1839–1911).

'Polyphonic Motets', as motets were, by definition, polyphonic. The consensus is that this was a mistake by Watson, who commented that the work has 'since been printed for private circulation, and is said by experts to be the last word on the subject.'

Watson's best description of Holmes's 'melancholy wailings' came during their first encounter in Baker Street in *A Study in Scarlet* where the latter's skills on the violin are described as:

> … very remarkable, but as eccentric as all his other accomplishments. That he could play pieces, and difficult pieces, I knew well, because at my request he has played me some of Mendelssohn's Lieder, and other favourites. When left to himself, however, he would seldom produce any music or attempt any recognized air. Leaning back in his armchair of an evening, he would close his eyes and scrape carelessly at the fiddle which was thrown across his knee. Sometimes the chords were sonorous and melancholy. Occasionally they were fantastic and cheerful. Clearly they reflected the thoughts which possessed him, but whether the music aided those thoughts, or whether the playing was simply the result of a whim or fancy, was more than I could determine. I might have rebelled against these exasperating solos had it not been that he usually terminated them by playing in quick succession a whole series of my favourite airs as a slight compensation for the trial upon my patience.

According to Watson in 'The Red-Headed League', Holmes was 'not only a very capable performer, but a composer of no ordinary merit'. The detective certainly seems to have loved his music, as this passage continues, observing him listening to music:

> All the afternoon he sat in the stalls wrapped in the most perfect happiness, gently waving his long, thin fingers in time to the music, while his gently smiling face and his languid, dreamy eyes were as unlike those of Holmes, the sleuth-hound, Holmes the relentless, keen-witted, ready-handed criminal agent, as it was possible to conceive. In his singular character the dual nature alternately asserted itself, and his extreme exactness and astuteness represented, as I have often thought, the reaction against the poetic and contemplative mood which occasionally predominated in him. The swing of his nature took him

from extreme languor to devouring energy; and, as I knew well, he was never so truly formidable as when, for days on end, he had been lounging in his armchair amid his improvisations and his black-letter editions. Then it was that the lust of the chase would suddenly come upon him, and that his brilliant reasoning power would rise to the level of intuition, until those who were unacquainted with his methods would look askance at him as on a man whose knowledge was not that of other mortals. When I saw him that afternoon so enwrapped in the music at St James's Hall I felt that an evil time might be coming upon those whom he had set himself to hunt down.

It is not certain what the music was on this occasion, or indeed who performed it. Perhaps it was Holmes's favourite violinist, the Moravian-born Wilma Norman-Neruda (1839–1911), who flourished during his formative years. He refers to the 'magnificence' of her 'bowing', noting particularly its 'attack', in *A Study in Scarlet*. She went on to marry Charles Hallé the German-born pianist who founded the Manchester-based orchestra which bore his name.

It is clear that Holmes used music as a form not just of relaxation, but of mental recuperation, which was essential in his work. So, in 'The Adventure of the Mazarin Stone', when he needed to give the villainous Count Negretto Sylvius time to reflect, he retired to his bedroom to play 'that most haunting of tunes', the Hoffmann 'Barcarole' – more specifically, the barcarolle from *Les Contes d'Hoffmann* by Jacques Offenbach.

Offenbach was French, but generally Holmes's taste tended to German composers. He hurries to an unnamed opera by Richard Wagner after resolving 'The Adventure of the Red Circle' earlier than he had thought (thus enabling him to hear the second act). And he invites Watson to *Les Huguenots*, an opera by Giacomo Meyerbeer, after solving the mystery of *The Hound of the Baskervilles*. In this context he mentioned the De Reszkes, a prolific musical family, featuring the siblings Jean (tenor), Édouard (bass), and Joséphine (soprano), who often played in this particular piece at the Royal Opera House throughout the 1880s.

And then there was Irene Adler, the minx who outfoxed him in 'A Scandal in Bohemia'. American born, she was a retired contralto who had sung at La Scala and the Imperial Opera in Warsaw. Despite Holmes's pathological lack of emotional commitment, she remained 'always the woman'.

When it came to the visual arts, Holmes, with his pedigree in that field, was well-informed, if not notably

Above 'All afternoon he sat in the stalls', Sidney Paget's 1891 illustration for 'The Adventure of the Red-Headed League'.

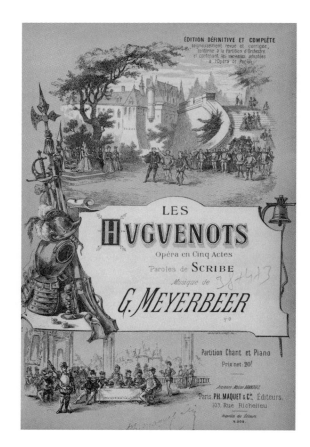

enthusiastic. His knowledge of the French artist Jean
Baptiste Greuze proved helpful in his investigation into
the supposed murder of John Douglas in *The Valley of Fear*.
Holmes suspected the hand of his arch-enemy Professor
Moriarty in the affair. But Inspector Macdonald from
Scotland Yard was not so sure. He said he had been to see
the professor and had found him very respectable. When
Holmes asked him if this interview had taken place in the
professor's study, the inspector said it had. And did he see
the painting there? asked Holmes. Yes, indeed, replied
Macdonald. But did he know it was by Greuze, who
flourished between 1750 and 1800? When the inspector
showed some impatience with this line of discussion,
Holmes convinced him of its relevance by telling him that
a painting by Greuze had sold for more than £40,000 in
1865. The inference was, how could a supposedly modest
professor, whose income could not have topped
£700 per annum, have afforded such a work? Ergo,
there must have been something fishy about him.

Holmes uses his knowledge of the decorative arts to
trap Baron Adelbert Gruner, a murderer and serial
seducer, who has taken the daughter of General de
Merville 'of Khyber fame' in thrall in 'The Adventure

of the Illustrious Client'. The only way to disabuse her of her
fantasy about this man is to get hold of the book (his 'lust
diary') in which he lists all his female conquests. Knowing
that Gruner likes to collect Chinese pottery, Holmes enlists
Watson's aid. This requires him to take a quick course
in Chinese ceramics, which means going to the London
Library, taking out a number of books and spending most
of the night and the next morning acquiring a patina of
knowledge on the subject. Watson recalled, 'There I learned
of the hall-marks of the great artist-decorators, of the mystery
of cyclical dates, the marks of the Hung-wu and the beauties
of the Yung-lo, the writings of Tang-ying, and the glories of
the primitive period of the Sung and the Yuan.' Holmes then
gives Watson a delicate piece of Ming pottery, asks him to
pose as a seller and offer it to Gruner as part of a collection.
This way he can gain entry into the Baron's house and enable
Holmes to find the incriminating book. As Holmes tells
Watson, 'No finer piece ever passed through Christie's.
A complete set of this would be worth a king's ransom –
in fact, it is doubtful if there is a complete set outside the
imperial palace of Peking. The sight of this would drive
a real connoisseur wild.' Indeed, this is true. Gruner is
distracted and Holmes is able to get the details he wants.

Above A Great Picture Sale at Christies, *illustration by Sydney Prior Hall (1842–1922).*

Opposite The front cover of Punch *magazine, 7 May 1941. The 1849 illustration by Richard Doyle (1824–83) was used for over a century.*

Unusually, Holmes seemed to regard artistic achievement as evidence not simply of a complex mind, but also of criminal potential. He recalled that his old friend Charlie Peace (otherwise not identified, but clearly a villain) was a violin virtuoso, while the real-life forger and possible killer, Thomas Griffiths Wainewright, was, in his estimation in 'The Adventure of the Illustrious Client', 'no mean artist'.

The same could be said of Holmes in his professional capacity. He liked to stress his powers of dogged deduction, but he was also an artist. For along with his fiddle playing, he was a master of disguise. Commenting on his transformation into a non-Conformist clergyman in *A Study in Scarlet*, Watson noted, 'His expression, his manner, his very soul seemed to vary with every fresh part that he assumed. The stage lost a fine actor, even as science lost an acute reasoner, when he became a specialist in crime.' The detective adopted other disguises not just in the story, but throughout the canon, from the sailor Captain Basil in 'The Adventure of Black Peter', to an elderly woman in 'The Adventure of the Mazarin Stone', not to mention an Irish American spy called Altamont in *His Last Bow*.

Conan Doyle certainly couldn't match Holmes's musical knowledge. However, he did master the playing of a strange brass instrument called a bombardon when he was studying at

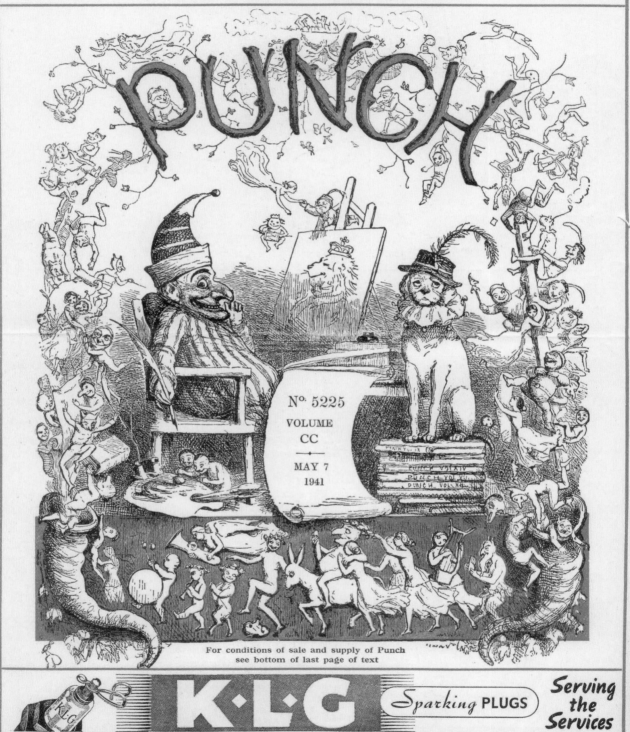

No. 5225

VOLUME
CC

MAY 7
1941

For conditions of sale and supply of Punch
see bottom of last page of text

Registered at the General Post Office as a Newspaper.　Entered as second-class Mail Matter at the New York, N.Y., Post Office, 1903.　Subscription, inclusive of Extra Numbers: Inland Postage 30/- per annum (15/- six months); Overseas, 36/6 per annum (Canada, 34/- per annum).　Postage of this issue: Great Britain and Ireland, 1½d.; Canada, 1d. Elsewhere Overseas, 1d.

Feldkirch, a Jesuit school in Austria, during his 'gap year' between Stonyhurst College and Edinburgh University. He recalled in his memoirs how he had played in public – 'good music, too, "Lohengrin," and "Tannhauser," – within a week or two of my first lesson, but they pressed me on for the occasion and the Bombardon, as it was called, only comes in on a measured rhythm with an occasional run, which sounds like a hippopotamus doing a step-dance.'

As for Conan Doyle's credentials in the visual arts, they were largely hereditary. He didn't personally acquire any great talent, but he had plenty of artists among his close relations. Having come to London from his native Dublin in the 1820s, his grandfather, John Doyle, had built up a formidable reputation as an artist, notably, under the name H.B., as a political caricaturist. At least three of John's sons were artists. The best known was Richard (or Dicky), Arthur Conan Doyle's uncle, who not only picked up his father's gift as an illustrator and caricaturist (he drew the sketch which acted as the cover image for *Punch* magazine for over a century), but who was also a celebrated artist in his own right, best known for his painting of fairies (a modish subject at the time). Another uncle, Henry, also painted before becoming director of Ireland's National

Gallery for almost a quarter of a century. And even Conan Doyle's father, Charles, was something of an artist, contributing drawings to his son's works (including images of a bearded Sherlock Holmes for the 1887 edition of *A Study in Scarlet*). However, he didn't have the family flair and was sent to Scotland to work as a clerk in the Office of Works in Edinburgh. Charles's second name was Altamont, which opens up a variety of Freudian interpretations of that spy in *His Last Bow*.

One thing is clear – Holmes channelled a considerable appreciation of art into his calling as a detective.

Below A Dance around the Moon, *watercolour on paper, by Charles Altamont Doyle (1832–93).*

A FEW
ATHLETIC TASTES

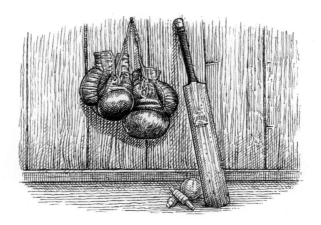

The traditional image of Sherlock Holmes poring over a 'three-pipe problem' in his Baker Street rooms, having just injected himself with a 7 per cent solution of cocaine, doesn't suggest an athletic or even a particularly energetic man. But while not as great an enthusiast for sport as his creator Arthur Conan Doyle, the fictional detective denizen of Baker Street was fit, agile and a master of a range of physical activities.

It's true that Holmes had little aptitude for team sports in the manner of Conan Doyle. Not having been educated, so far as is known, at a public school (though he may have gone to Oxford, or another, university), he hadn't been brought up to the tunes and daily habits of Victorian-style, muscular Christianity. He was more of an individual. When consulted by the distraught captain of the Cambridge University rugby team about the disappearance of his star player in 'The Adventure of the Missing Three-Quarter', Holmes has not only never heard of this man, who was obviously well known as he had been capped for England, but he also makes clear he has never had any interest in that type of pursuit. 'My ramifications stretch out into many sections of society,' he avers, 'but never, I am happy to say, into amateur sport', which,

for some reason, he goes on to describe as 'the best and soundest thing in England'.

Conan Doyle was very different. He attended Stonyhurst College, a Roman Catholic public school in Lancashire with a strong rugby football tradition. But his passion was the game of cricket, even if he wasn't particularly good at it at school, only playing in the second eleven. At university he boxed a bit. It wasn't until he started working as a GP in Portsmouth that he turned his attention to the sports field. He was one of the founders of Portsmouth Football Association Club which (although the line was not direct) was a forerunner of the Portsmouth Football Club; for some time in the twenty-first century Portsmouth FC played in the English Premier League. He seems to have been a versatile player, sometimes appearing as a full back, sometimes as a goalkeeper, often under the *nom de jeu*, A.C. Smith. During this period (the 1880s) he also began playing regular cricket, initially for local elevens and later, for the next quarter of a century, for leading amateur sides, including the Marylebone Cricket Club (MCC). When he moved to Hindhead in Surrey in the mid-1890s he turned out for nearby villages and also for his own scratch team, which he liked to entertain after matches at his house, Undershaw. He also founded the Authors Cricket Club, made up of writers such as P.G. Wodehouse and Conan Doyle's brother-in-law E.W. Hornung, the creator of the Raffles stories. (The team continues to this day, with this present author a member.)

In 1901 Conan Doyle achieved what he regarded as the summit of his cricketing career. Bowling for the MCC against the London County team at Crystal Palace, he managed to dismiss W.G. Grace, who was regarded as the greatest batsman of his age. He was so excited that he wrote a poem about his experience titled 'A Reminiscence of Cricket', which began:

Once in my heyday of cricket
Oh, day I shall ever recall!
I captured that glorious wicket,
The greatest, the grandest all.

Sherlock Holmes was more reticent about his markedly different sporting skills. One of the first things the reader learns about him in *A Study in Scarlet* is that he is, in Dr Watson's words, 'an expert singlestick player, boxer, and swordsman'.

The least known of these accomplishments today is singlestick. This was a primitive form of sparring using a stick, usually made of ash. It had enjoyed considerable popularity in the eighteenth and early nineteenth century, when it was patronized by royalty. It was still a well-known sport in the mid-1800s, when it is mentioned in *Tom Brown's Schooldays*. But by the end of the century, it was being superseded by the épée and modern fencing. Although there was still enough interest for it to be included as an event (for the first and only time) in the 1904 Olympics.

Although Holmes's expertise in this sport is first mentioned by Dr Watson, the detective refers to it himself after he has apparently been beaten up outside the Café Royal while investigating the case in 'The Adventure of the Illustrious Client'. When Watson comes to visit him at home in Baker Street, Holmes tells him his injuries are not as bad as they might seem, and adds, 'I'm a bit of a singlestick expert, as you know. I took most of (the blows) on my guard. It was the second man that was too much for me.'

Holmes's forte was not singlestick but boxing, which not only kept him fit, but which also introduced

Left Illustration from The Strand Magazine *in 1909 depicting Conan Doyle being dismissed by what he described as 'the most singular ball that I have ever received'.*

Opposite top The Football Match *(1890), colour lithograph, by William Heysham Overend (1851–98.*

Opposite bottom A Cricket Match *(1852), oil on canvas, by W.J. Bowden.*

"A STRAIGHT LEFT AGAINST A SLOGGING RUFFIAN."

Opposite '*A straight left against a slogging ruffian*', *Sidney Paget's 1904 illustration for* '*The Adventure of the Solitary Cyclist*'.

Left Two photographs published in Pearson's Magazine *(February 1901) illustrating Dr Edward Barton-Wright's method of disabling an opponent taller than yourself.*

him to a group of sportsmen with special skills that he was able to call on for his professional purposes. This was clear early in his career in *The Sign of Four* when he visited Bartholomew Sholto who employed a doorman-cum-bodyguard called McMurdo who had once fought with Holmes in the boxing ring. Their history of mutual sparring meant the detective was part of a sporting inner circle, which was enough to gain him immediate entrance to Sholto.

The meeting is amusingly recounted by Conan Doyle, or Watson, if you prefer. McMurdo initially refuses entry to the detective and his companion, saying he doesn't know them. Holmes puts him right. 'Oh, yes you do, McMurdo … I don't think you can have forgotten me. Don't you remember that amateur who fought three rounds with you at Alison's rooms on the night of your benefit four years back?' The prize-fighter is astounded. 'Not Mr Sherlock Holmes!' he roars. 'God's truth! how could I have mistook you? If instead o' standin' there so quiet you had just stepped up and given me that cross-hit of yours under the jaw, I'd ha' known you without a question. Ah, you're one that has wasted your gifts, you have! You might have aimed high, if you had joined the

fancy.' Holmes notes wryly, 'You see, Watson, if all else fails me, I have still one of the scientific professions open to me.' And of course he gains entry.

But Holmes was not interested in putting his pugilism to any personal advantage. As Watson remarks of him in 'The Adventure of the Yellow Face':

> Few men were capable of greater muscular effort, and he was undoubtedly one of the finest boxers of his weight that I have ever seen; but he looked upon aimless bodily exertion as a waste of energy, and he seldom bestirred himself save where there was some professional object to be served.

One example of him putting his physical skills to good purpose was the use he made of the Japanese-style martial art of baritsu when confronted by his arch-enemy Professor Moriarty at the Reichenbach Falls. This was a thinly disguised (or perhaps wrongly remembered) version of bartitsu, a system of self-defence invented by Dr Edward Barton-Wright, a British engineer who had spent many years in Japan. Its appellation mixed Barton-Wright's surname with jujitsu, the Japanese so-called 'gentle art'

of appearing to yield to the moves of an opponent, and then controlling them. He expounded on his invention in his article 'The New Art of Self-Defence' (which was published in two parts in *Pearson's Magazine* in March and April 1899), and he subsequently established a school in London's Shaftesbury Avenue, which taught his techniques. The establishment did not last long; within three years it had folded. But these years coincided with Conan Doyle showing considerable interest in body improvement, having adopted the body-building and healthy-living regime of the celebrated German-born strong-man Eugen Sandow in 1898. The dating causes excitement among dedicated Sherlockians: the story 'The Adventure of the Empty House', which mentions Holmes's use of bartitsu in his clash with Moriarty, was first published in *Collier's* and *The Strand Magazine* in September and October 1903. It looked back to the two men's fight to the death in Switzerland in May 1891, as initially reported in the story 'The Final Problem', published in December 1893. How, ask the Sherlockians, could Holmes have used bartitsu in 1891 when it wasn't announced to the world for another eight years? One theory (summarized by Leslie S. Klinger in *The New Annotated Sherlock Holmes*) is that Holmes had actually studied jujitsu

and Watson, having recently read Barton-Wright's articles on bartitsu, muddled the two skills. It has also been noted that since learning jujitsu takes at least seven years, Holmes must have been an adept since 1883 or 1884.

The only sports in which Holmes personally admits some proficiency are fencing and boxing (mentioned thus in 'The Adventure of the Gloria Scott' – where he acknowledges that, bar these two, 'I had few athletic tastes'). He also clearly has some knowledge of racing, as indicated in 'The Adventure of Silver Blaze' (Dr Watson perhaps more so, since when, in 'The Adventure of Shoscombe Old Place', he is asked if he knows anything about racing, he replies that he ought to since half his war-wound pension goes to subsidizing it). But Holmes is never actually seen in the saddle. And he never participates in any ball games.

Conan Doyle, as indicated, was very different. He loved everything about sport. And although sporting ability was coveted at the time as evidence of manliness (and, by extension, of commitment to the virility and spirit of adventure that went with military prowess and running an empire), these were not overriding factors for him. He did however tell his mother in 1899 that he had 'perhaps

Opposite Eugen Sandow (1867–1925), known as 'the father of modern bodybuilding'.

Right Sidney Paget's 1892 illustration of the racehorse Silver Blaze.

Above Tattenham Corner, the Epsom Derby, *coloured chalks on paper, by Gilbert Holiday (1879–1937).*

Opposite Conan Doyle at the wheel *of his 16 hp Dietrich-Lorraine motorcar competing in the Prince Henry Tour in 1911.*

the strongest influence over young men, particularly young athletic sporting men, of anyone in England, bar Kipling'. But he was trying to calm her worries about him going
to South Africa to fight in the Boer War. And it is clear from his boxing stories *The Croxley Master* and *Rodney Stone* that, although he saw sport as patriotic, it was also about the British sense of fair play. At root, he simply marvelled at the way that sport brought out the best qualities in human beings.

He proved this through his participation in an extraordinarily wide range of sports. As well as his cricketing and footballing feats, he competed in the English Amateur Billiards Championship, reaching the third round in 1913. As a young man he often liked to box for fun; in 1880, while working as a locum doctor on the whaling ship SS *Hope*, he earned the admiration of the crew's Steward Jack Lamb for his performance in a makeshift boxing ring. Lamb described him as 'the best sur-r-r-geon we ever had … he's blacked my e'e.' Later, after boxing had featured in his *Rodney Stone* (and other) stories, he was a regular visitor to the National Sporting Club, where regulated professional prize fights

were held. As a result of this interest, he was asked to referee the World Professional Boxing championship fight between James Jefferies and Jack Johnson in Reno, Nevada, in 1909. He loved golf, and was captain of the Crowborough Beacon golf club near Windlesham, his final home. He was for many years a dedicated skier, travelling regularly with his family to the Alps, where he is often credited, somewhat extravagantly, with introducing downhill competitive skiing. In the years running up to the First World War he participated in the promotion of the Olympic Games. This stemmed, in part, from his involvement in the Olympics in London in 1908; after attending as a journalist, he raised money for Dorando Pietri, the Italian marathon runner who missed out on the gold medal after being disqualified for receiving assistance from the umpires in the final stages of the race.

And that's not to forget Conan Doyle's interest in other fringe activities, such as shooting (though he was adamant he didn't believe in killing animals or birds), flying, and motor sport (competing in his 16 hp Dietrich Lorraine in the Prince Henry Tour, a celebrated motor rally, in Germany and Britain in July 1911).

As he wrote in *Memories and Adventures* towards the end of his life:

On the whole as I look back there is no regret in my mind for the time that I have devoted to sport. It gives health and strength, but above all it gives a certain balance of mind without which a man is not complete. To give and to take, to accept success modestly and defeat bravely, to fight against odds, to stick to one's point, to give credit to your enemy and value your friend – these are some of the lessons which true sport should impart.

Left above Conan Doyle playing the winning stroke in the second round of the English Amateur Billiards Championship, 1913.

Right above Dorando Pietri staggers over the finishing line of the marathon at the 1908 London Olympics.

Left below Conan Doyle playing golf at Le Touquet.

Right below Conan Doyle posing on skis in the Alps.

STAYING
THE COURSE

Over the past hundred years or so, scholars, fans and publishers of various kinds have vied with the Conan Doyle estate to ensure that Sherlock Holmes remains a subject of fascination.

Ronald Knox, a Classics don at Trinity College, Oxford, kick-started the serious business of being a Sherlockian with a talk to a small group called the Bodley Club in nearby Merton College on 10 March 1911. Over the previous two decades, parodies and other spin-offs had already given a lively send-off to Holmes's afterlife. These were mainly literary creations, starting with J.M. Barrie's 'My Evening with Sherlock Holmes', which appeared in *The Speaker* in November 1891, four months after the publication of 'A Scandal in Bohemia'. The flow of spoofs continued, with the Canadian Robert Barr's 'The Great Pegram Mystery' in *The Idler* magazine in 1892, which featured a detective called Sherlaw Kombs with such a disdain for Scotland Yard that he made a point of never visiting Scotland. A particularly prolific contributor was the American writer John Kendrick Bangs, who brought Holmes and the character Raffles together in *R. Holmes & Co.: Being the Remarkable Adventures of Raffles Holmes, Esq., Detective and Amateur Cracksman by Birth* (1906). This had Holmes, the

amateur detective, pursuing Raffles, the gentleman thief who had appeared in books by Conan Doyle's brother-in-law E.W. Hornung, and falling in love with his daughter, by whom he has a son, Raffles Holmes, who was well set up for his own investigative adventures. But Knox expanded the world of Holmes by bringing together erudition and wit in a unique manner that has helped the cult of the detective to endure ever since. He himself came from a suitably distinguished background – the son of the Bishop of Manchester, his siblings were Edmund (or E.V., the editor of *Punch*, who was known professionally by his pseudonym Evoe), Dillwyn (Dilly, a classical scholar who became chief cryptanalyst at Bletchley Park during the Second World War), and Wilfred (a priest and theologian).

In his Bodley Club paper, 'The Mind and Art of Sherlock Holmes', Ronald Knox addressed the Holmes oeuvre with the precise textual exegesis of a German Biblical scholar and the soft humour of his witty contemporaries. The club members loved it, and added their own commentaries. Knox gave the talk a couple more times before publishing it as an essay in a short-lived undergraduate review, the *Blue Book*, in July 1912. Conan Doyle liked this, and sent a letter of appreciation which expanded on several points,

noting that he had never given Watson anything clever to say as this would have destroyed his image as a bumbler. Ever sensitive to accusations of plagiarism, he also pointed out that Holmes's sojourn in 'Thibet' (chronicled in 'The Adventure of the Empty House') was not copied, as Knox had suggested, from the travels of Dr Nikola, a Moriarty-type villain who appeared in the works of the Australian author Guy Boothby in 1890s, but was his own invention.

Knox established the idea that Sherlock Holmes was special, someone to be studied and celebrated, albeit in a light-hearted manner. Sherlockian studies were born, not as an academic discipline, but as a game to be played with the conceit that Holmes and Watson were real. Watson was Holmes's biographer, and Conan Doyle merely his agent. The canon was a record of this couple's lives, to be pored over for details such as the detective's parentage and places of education (was he an Oxford or Cambridge man?) – matters that could be endlessly debated over a drink or dinner.

Knox's interest in detective fiction led him to become a member of the (invitation-only) Detection Club, a gathering place for many of the authors, such as Agatha Christie, who contributed to the post-war golden age of detective

fiction. In editing *The Best Detective Stories* of 1928, he wrote an introduction that set out the precepts for writing detective fiction that came to be known as the 'Ten Commandments' of the craft. While not specifically Sherlockian, these drew on his deep knowledge of the canon to suggest various rules, including one clearly followed by Holmes (all supernatural and preternatural agencies are ruled out as a matter of course); one not so clearly (not more than one secret room or passage is allowable); and one, doubtless tongue in cheek, which could hardly be committed to paper today (no Chinaman must figure in the story).

The death of Conan Doyle in July 1930, along with the official opening of the Detection Club at much the same time, sparked renewed interest in Sherlockian matters. For the first time, the detective's colleague seemed worthy of examination in a volume published the following year titled *Dr Watson: Prolegomena to the study of a biographical problem* by S.C. Roberts (later Sir Sydney Roberts, master of Pembroke College, Cambridge). *Sherlock Holmes, Fact or Fiction* by the British alpinist T.S. Blakeney appeared in 1932; and *The Private Life of Sherlock Holmes* by Vincent Starrett in 1933. Reviews of these books and related queries were published in the *Saturday Review of Literature* in New York, a weekly journal which had been founded by (amongst others) the journalist, clubman and Holmes aficionado Christopher Morley. In a piece for the *Saturday Review of Literature* in 1933, Morley suggested from his reading of the canon that Sherlock Holmes had been born on 6 January. He and some friends decided to meet on that date for a cocktail party at the Hotel Duane where it seems that the idea of the Baker Street Irregulars (BSI) was first mooted. A constitution and various rules (including a stipulation that the first toast should always be to 'the woman') was drawn up. A follow-up dinner was held on 5 July, and then re-formulated as an annual event on 6 January 1936, since when it has indeed been held on as near as possible to that date every year.

The BSI, the first dedicated Sherlockian society, was soon followed by others, so that today (almost a century later) there are hundreds (around 340 according to one recent listing) of related or scion societies. These include the Bootmakers of Toronto, the Speckled Band of Boston and the Norwegian Explorers of Minnesota, as well as the Sherlock Holmes Society of London, which holds a special place as it is situated in the city where the detective lived and worked. Since the original BSI was male only, women had to fight to join this American based gathering. One or two crept in, including Conan Doyle's daughter, Dame Jean.

Opposite above Ronald Knox (1888–1957), Catholic priest, classicist, theologian and early Sherlockian.

Opposite below Merton College, Oxford, where Ronald Knox addressed the Bodley Club.

Above Agatha Christie (1890–1976), one of the founder members of the Detection Club.

Above Members of the Sherlock Holmes Society of London gather before a week-long tour of Switzerland in the footsteps of their hero, 4 April 1968.

But most women were excluded and so a group set up their own society, the Adventuresses of Sherlock Holmes (ASH), which had its origins in the 1960s in a private Catholic university, Albertus Magnus (close to Yale in New Haven, Connecticut). For twenty-five years ASH determinedly held its own dinners at the same time as the BSI's. In 1991, its members, led by its founder Evelyn Herzog, were finally invited to join the BSI. Since then, several more societies for women have been formed, including the Baker Street Babes, which was responsible for the first all-female blog in 2011.

The British Sherlock Holmes Society, with the crime writer Dorothy Sayers a member, was established in London in 1934 in the wake of the BSI's arrival. (It was Sayers who came up with the adage that the Sherlockian game 'must be played as solemnly as a country county cricket match at Lord's.) However, this initial group was put into abeyance during the Second World War, and the new (and still existing) Sherlock Holmes Society of London (SHSL) was reconstituted in 1951, following a major exhibition on the detective and his creator at Abbey House (the Art Deco headquarters of the Abbey National Building Society), which had become identified as the site of 221B Baker Street. The exhibition was staged by the then St Marylebone Borough Council as its

Above Dorothy L. Sayers (1893–1957) in the Detection Club on Gerrard Street, 1939.

Left Abbey House, the former London headquarters of the Abbey National Building Society, stands on what is often claimed to be the original site of 221B Baker Street.

principal contribution to the celebration of the Festival of Britain that year. The first President of the SHSL was Sir Sydney Roberts, one of the pioneers in Sherlockian studies twenty years earlier.

The exhibition stimulated several initiatives to promote Baker Street and its corner of Marylebone as the physical centre for Sherlockian studies. Having allowed its building to be used for the 1951 exhibition, Abbey National made efforts to expand on this association. Since letters were often written to Sherlock Holmes at its address, it began to employ a secretary to answer this correspondence, which at its height ran to 700 items a year, ranging from requests from children about how to deal with their teachers to queries about crimes and mysteries such as the Loch Ness Monster. In 1985 the Holmes scholar Richard Lancelyn Green published a selection of these letters.

A feature of the 1951 exhibition had been a full-scale representation of Sherlock Holmes's sitting room at Baker Street, complete with details from the canon such as the violin, pipes and chemistry equipment. In subsequent years, this Sherlockian room toured various venues before, in 1957, it was bought by the Whitbread brewing company to feature in the refurbishment of its pub, the Northumberland Arms

Below **The sitting room of 221B Baker Street, as it was reconstructed as part of the Sherlock Holmes Society of London exhibition in 1951.**

Opposite **The exterior of the successful, though controversial Sherlock Holmes Museum, at 239 Baker Street.**

in Northumberland Avenue near Trafalgar Square. This hostelry was referred to in the story 'The Adventure of the Noble Bachelor' in 1892. Whitbread recreated at least part of the Baker Street room in a corner of the revamped pub.

In 1990 a museum was opened in a Georgian house just north of Abbey House at 239 Baker Street, which it claimed was the true site of Sherlock Holmes's lodging at 221B Baker Street. (The reality is more complicated. There hadn't been a 221B Baker Street in Sherlock Holmes's or Conan Doyle's days. This section of the street was then known as Upper Baker Street; after this name was discontinued in the 1930s the numbers were redistributed so that the Abbey National headquarters stood at 215 to 229 Baker Street, thus incorporating 221B.) This new enterprise proved popular with tourists, as the only place in London, certainly the only museum, where they could explore the life and times of Sherlock Holmes. It too had its replica of the interior of the detective's house, and, as a commercial venture, it sold a lot of related merchandise. But the museum proved controversial. It was soon at loggerheads with its building society neighbour as to where the Sherlock Holmes correspondence should be delivered. It claimed that uncertainty on this matter prevented it from setting up a mail-order business which

would give it proper financial viability. This dispute mouldered on for many years until 2002 when, with the building society about to be taken over by the Spanish bank Santander, Abbey National vacated its site on Baker Street.

There was no love lost either between the museum and the Conan Doyle estate, which was opposed to any suggestion that Sherlock Holmes was a real person. The museum continued to make news as a result of protracted legal disputes involving its owners; it emerged from various court hearings was that the museum was a lucrative enterprise. And Holmes himself remained undeniably popular. Maintaining the detective's local connections were an 11 foot- (3.5-metre) high bronze statue of him by John Doubleday (unveiled in a prominent position outside Baker Street station in 1999) and a hotel bearing his name in neighbouring Chiltern Street.

Attempts have been made to recreate Holmes's environment in other locations. A replica of the detective's Baker Street room was built in the Swiss town of Lucens, near Lausanne, where Conan Doyle's son Adrian had lived in a castle. After his death in 1970, the museum was run by the Lucens municipality. Also in Switzerland, there is a gallery close to the Reichenbach Falls, which boasts another statue by John Doubleday. And that's just the beginning.

In all, according to Brian Pugh's invaluable *A Chronology of the Life of Sir Arthur Conan Doyle*, seventy-three statues or plaques around the world commemorate either Holmes or Conan Doyle, including one of the detective and Dr Watson in Moscow (on the Smolenskaya Embankment, near the British Embassy), unveiled in April 2007. London isn't the only city with a Sherlock Holmes pub either. There are drinking places of that name in Bordeaux (France), Melbourne (Australia), and three in Edmonton (Canada) owned by the Sherlock Holmes Hospitality Group, which has been in business since 1985. Fittingly for the birthplace of the author, Edinburgh has a pub called The Conan Doyle.

Along this journey, as Sherlock Holmes has steadily emerged as a brand, various centres for Sherlockian studies have developed. An important stimulus was the sale at Christie's in 2004 of the assets of the Conan Doyle estate, including several of the author's original manuscripts, letters and notebooks. This followed the death of Dame Jean Conan Doyle, the last of Sir Arthur's children, in November 1997. She had brought some stability to the estate's affairs after the excesses of her brothers Denis and Adrian, who had frittered the estate's assets away, before dying relatively young in 1955 and 1970.

The Christie's sale helped disperse some of this material to a new network of centres of Sherlockian study. Several important items found their way to the British Library. Others were snapped up for private collections, notably those of Costa Rossakis and Glen Miranker in the United States. Both men have been generous in granting access to their holdings and in lending them out. Miranker put together a well-received exhibition of his material at the Grolier Club in New York in 2022. This included parts of the manuscript of *The Hound of the Baskervilles*, an original magazine copy of *A Study in Scarlet*, and a selection of his many pirated editions of Sherlock Holmes. These were the versions (often cheap and garish) put out largely by American publishers in the detective's early years in order to circumvent copyright legislation, as codified internationally in the Berne Convention for the Protection of Literary and Artistic Works, signed in 1886. US copyright law at the time did not apply to authors who were not citizens or residents. Although this was rectified in the International Copyright Act of 1891, pirating continued into the early years of the twentieth century, and the US did not actually sign the Convention until 1989.

The practice of pirating was helped by the US Postal Service; although letters cost 2 cents each to post, periodicals

Opposite The Sherlock Holmes statue by John Doubleday (1947–), unveiled outside Baker Street Underground station in 1999.

Left A monument to Holmes and Watson stands near the British Embassy in Moscow.

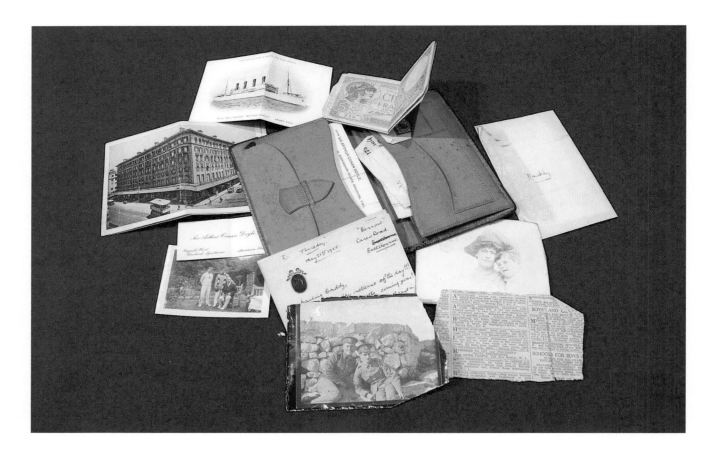

were carried for 1 cent. So, the pirates adopted all sorts of ruses to pass their books off as magazines, issuing them as part of a library or a numbered series, and so on.

The Christie's sale had one very unfortunate consequence, as it was linked to the death of Richard Lancelyn Green, the world's foremost Sherlock Holmes scholar. He was convinced that his friend Dame Jean wanted to donate her estate, with its Sherlockian pickings, to the British public. His agitation on learning that most would be sold privately may well have contributed to him taking his own life. However, he in turn bequeathed his unrivalled collection of Holmes material to the city of Portsmouth, where Conan Doyle had worked as a doctor in the 1880s. As a result, Portsmouth's museum and library have become significant centres of Sherlockian study.

For a while, there was a plan to develop another nearby spot with Conan Doyle associations along these lines. This was the author's house, Undershaw, in Hindhead, Surrey, which he had built himself in 1896–97. After he moved to Sussex in 1908, it was used as a hotel. Interested parties tried to put together a bid when the premises came up for sale in 2013 in the hope of establishing a Holmesian hub there. But the funding proved elusive, and it was decided

– probably wisely – that there were sufficient centres of excellence dedicated to the detective elsewhere.

Another possible location of Sherlockian interest was Conan Doyle's native Edinburgh. But it was slow to capitalize on its connection to the author. A bronze statue of Sherlock Holmes was erected close to the author's birthplace in Picardy Place in 1991. But, since then, it has regularly been shrouded or dismantled as a result of endless traffic works. Other places in the city with possible claims include the National Library of Scotland, which was given the original manuscript of 'The Adventure of the Illustrious Client' in the will of Dame Jean Conan Doyle, and the Royal Colleges of both Physicians and Surgeons of Edinburgh, which have holdings relating to Conan Doyle's teacher, Dr Joseph Bell.

Meanwhile, buoyed by acquisitions from the Christie's sale and by additional donations, several places outside Britain developed into important centres of Sherlockian scholarship. The largest, with over 60,000 items, including manuscripts, journals and ephemera, 'through which' (to use its own words) 'the transformation of the Holmes character from the printed page to a cultural icon can be traced' is the Sherlock Holmes Collection at the University of Minnesota in Minneapolis. This has benefited from the gift, in the 1980s, of the holdings

*Opposite A collection of Conan
Doyle letters, photographs and other
items on sale at auction.*

*Above A exhibit at the Conan Doyle
Collection in Portsmouth.*

of John Bennett Shaw, perhaps the largest owner of Holmes material in the United States. The Toronto Public Library is also a significant repository, as is the Library at the University of Lausanne, which benefited from having Adrian Conan Doyle live close by for a number of years.

One thread running through the history of Sherlock Holmes is copyright, a matter which has been more fraught for such a well-known character than for most other literary figures. Until the 1980s the Holmes stories were protected in most territories under copyright for fifty to seventy years after the death of their author Arthur Conan Doyle in 1930. This period was increased in the UK and Europe to seventy years in 1995. Meanwhile the legislation in the United States was slightly different: a change there in the 1980s allowed copyrights to be extended for a certain time if they were renewed, and this period was further prolonged to seventy-five years from the date of a work's creation with Congressman Sonny Bono's copyright act of 1998 (the so-called Mickey Mouse Extension Act). As a result, ten stories from *The Casebook of Sherlock Holmes* (1923–7) remained under copyright in the US until the start of 2023.

This created a delicate situation. According to the law, the Conan Doyle estate, as the rights holder, was able to agree or decline requests to use this copyrighted material. In 2013 it decided to flex its muscles by insisting that Leslie Klinger, editor of the *New Annotated Sherlock Holmes* published in New York by W.W. Norton in 2005, should pay a licence fee on a proposed anthology of newly minted stories featuring the detective. The estate argued that this material showed Holmes as the more sociable and sympathetic personality found in the later, copyrighted stories rather than the brilliant but reclusive misanthrope found in the earlier tales – by then out of copyright. This line of reasoning threatened to halt further interpretations of Holmes, or at least delay them until the end of the latest period of copyright. Klinger decided to fight this, claiming essentially that the Holmes character was already formed before the later material came into play. The judge agreed, but not before the estate had attempted to halt other new versions of Holmes. In 2015 it sought to stop Miramax's film *Mr Holmes* on the grounds that, in depicting the detective

Below **The Arthur Conan Doyle Room at the Toronto Reference Library.**

Opposite Conan Doyle's son Adrian (left, 1910–70) plotting a new Sherlock Holmes story with mystery writer John Dickson Carr in 1952.

in his dotage, it used 'protected elements of setting, plot and character'. Five years later it employed a similar argument against Netflix's film *Enola Holmes*, which showed the detective working with his sister, Enola. It pursued not only the production company but also Nancy Springer, author of the young-adult series of books on which the film was based. The case went to court but was subsequently withdrawn.

Other companies, including the makers of both the Robert Downey Jr. (cinema) and Benedict Cumberbatch (TV) versions of Sherlock, accepted this situation and agreed to work with the Conan Doyle estate and pay the necessary licence fees. The legal framework was complicated by the fact that the estate copyrighted and sometimes patented various additional elements of the Holmes package, including use of the name Sherlock Holmes. A further confusing factor was that, for a while, there were two competing estates – the official one controlled by the Conan Doyle family, and another fronted by Andrea Reynolds Plunket, the widow of Sheldon Reynolds, the film director who had made a series of Sherlock Holmes films starring Ron Howard for television in the 1970s. With her family money, Plunket had bought the rights to the Sherlock Holmes stories from the widow of Denis Conan Doyle.

Until her death in 2016, Plunket continued to maintain ownership of them, often leading to further litigation. Often film companies and publishers (including Penguin), fearful of disruptive and expensive time in court, sought agreements with both claimants to the estate.

The invention of the World Wide Web from the early 1990s allowed users to access, to cut and paste, and generally to experiment with any version of a text, old or new, that they wanted. One result was a proliferation of fan fiction – stories written by enthusiasts conversant with the original texts and keen to expand on them in ways that amused them. Inevitably, well-known imaginary characters such as Batman, Mickey Mouse and Sherlock Holmes became important building blocks in the online phenomenon known as fan fiction (fanfic).

In fanfic no holds are barred. Indeed, every variety of interpretation is encouraged, partly because the medium allows – even dictates – it, and partly because this innovation coincided with another cultural development – the removal of traditional restrictions on matters of content, character and 'discourse' that followed the intellectual vogue for the post-structuralism of the French philosopher Roland Barthes. Together with his compatriot Michel

Foucault, he was particularly well known for identifying 'the death of the author', holding that the meaning of a 'text' came less from the author than the reader. The very idea of an 'author' suggested authority and paternalism. These concepts held significant sway in academia in the 1970s and 1980s before filtering through to popular culture.

The Sherlock Holmes stories were perhaps more open to reinterpretation along these lines than most, since his role in the canon is to be an authoritative know-all, an exemplar of the rationality of his age, and a white male one at that. Since the detective's business was to find meanings in hidden areas, why should not a critic or a reader seize upon his text and, using an associative rather than deductive logic, tease out gaps in the Holmes legend. (It is no coincidence that Holmes's technique is often described in terms of semiotics, the study of signs, which is the skill at the root of Barthes's structuralism.) That left opportunities for writers conversant with Conan Doyle's canon to open up, often teasingly and sympathetically, 'the Sherlock Holmes universe to alternative, possibly subversive, cultural and ideological codes', as the academic Ika Willis has put it.

One feature of fanfic has been to play with gender. Both Holmes and Watson have frequently been reinterpreted in the genre as women. Given their collaboration, their close relationship is inevitably much given to the 'ship' category of fan fiction (as in 'relationship'). Writers can ship characters, who become a ship or a pairing, sometimes with a pair name; in this couple's case, 'Johnlock', a reference which had an airing in the Sherlock series on BBC TV. Then there are varieties of ship, such as OTP (or One Time Pair) as a dedicated duo (or more) are often described. And that is before one gets into sub-genres, such as slash (which deals with same sex relationships) or het (which is determinedly heteronormative). Not surprisingly, Holmes and Watson often feature in slash. There have even been stories hinting at incest, with Sherlock having been abused by his elder brother Mycroft.

It is difficult to say exactly how many pieces of Sherlock Holmes fanfic have been published. By 2014, it seems, there were three quarters of a million such items about Harry Potter. J.K. Rowling, author of the Potter novels, is fairly relaxed about the phenomenon, though she (and Warner Brothers who produced the films) are opposed to stories with a violent or sexual content, arguing that children might stumble across them on the internet. Certain authors, such as George R.R. Martin, who wrote the *Game of Thrones*

books, and Anne Rice, of *The Vampire Chronicles*, adamantly dismiss fan fiction as infringement of copyright. In 2009, the heirs of J.D. Salinger managed to halt the publication of a book featuring an anachronistic seventy-six-year-old Holden Caulfield. But Rowling has made positive noises about fan fiction, and Stephenie Meyer (author of the vampire romance series *Twilight*) has encouraged it, even linking her website to choice pieces of fanfic.

By such benchmarks, the Conan Doyle estate has been reasonable in both its interpretation of the law, which hinges on the definition of 'fair use', and in its reading of the current social climate. It seems to have made a distinction between writings, usually books, which make their way onto cinema screens, where audiences can run into millions (with commensurate financial returns), and fan fiction, which is often published on websites and read by a handful of people.

One development has been the growth of cross referencing or intertextuality between mediums. (A modish way of describing this is archontic.) So, the *Sherlock* series on BBC television, itself a version of 'fandom' (or even 'fanon', the fan iteration of 'canon'), often played up connections (such as the Johnlock pairing), which had existed in the canon, but which had been amplified in fan fiction. ('Adlock' refers to a 'straight' pairing between Holmes and Irene Adler.) It was a two-way process, for fanfic also picked up ideas from TV; for example, in 'The Sign of Three' in the third BBC series, Mycroft phones Sherlock, asks if he remembers Redbeard, and his brother answers 'I'm not a child any more.' The name Redbeard then recurs in later episodes, as a dog, and even, cheekily, as a false memory.

This imitative approach to the canon stretches back to those early parodies, such as the one by J.M. Barrie, noted at the start. It includes unexpected contributions such as 'The Singularge Experience of Miss Anne Duffield', featuring Shamrock Womlbs, which appeared in John Lennon's book *A Spaniard in the Works* in June 1965. Lennon later described how, after reading one or two Holmes stories in his early years, he had been holed up for three months in a hotel in Tahiti where he found and devoured a collected edition of the stories. Conan Doyle himself, then his heirs, and now his estate, have been inclined to adopt a lenient attitude to such material, which generally serves to publicize the 'brand'.

Aspects of fandom can be expressed in different ways. For example, there is a long tradition of Sherlock Holmes comics. This reflects the strong visual tradition linked to

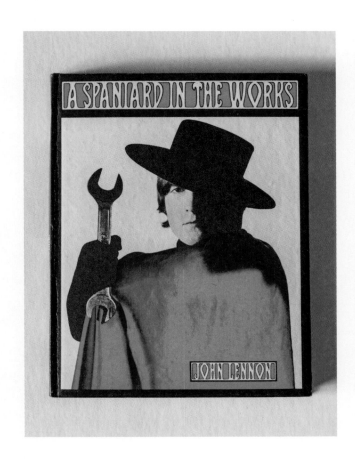

Opposite Fans in London attempt a Guinness World Record for the largest gathering of people dressed as Sherlock Holmes, 2014.

Above John Lennon's book A Spaniard in the Works *(1965) includes the Sherlock Holmes parody 'The Singularge Experience of Miss Anne Duffield'.*

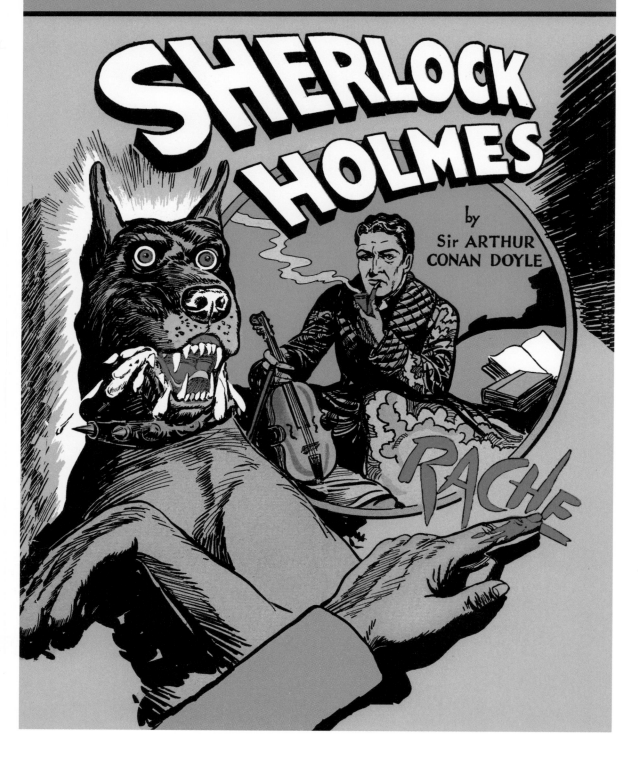

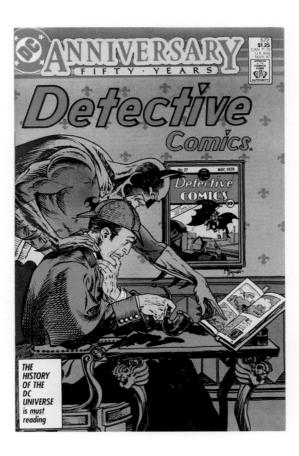

Opposite This 1947 issue of Classic Comics *contained adaptations of* A Study in Scarlet *and* The Hound of the Baskervilles, *with a suitably lurid cover illusrtation by H.C. Kiefer (1890–1957).*

Left In a special 50th anniversary issue of Detective Comics *from March 1987, a 135-year-old Holmes meets Batman.*

the detective, from the Paget drawings onwards. Sherlock Holmes first featured in comics in the 1930s when he made cameo appearances as a know-it-all sleuth who people consulted for professional advice. The first full-scale adaptation of a Holmes title in this genre – *The Sign of Four* – was published in 1944 as a supposedly instructive version of a definitive novel by *Classic Comics*. At the time *Classic Comics*, and its associated *Classics Illustrated*, had only been in business for three years as an imprint of the Eliot Publishing Company; it went through various incarnations until the series was discontinued in 1967. Another 'educational' title was *The Hound of the Baskervilles* from Look and Learn in 1967.

Comics were beginning to enter the media mainstream, with the market split between DC Comics (later a subsidiary of Warner Brothers), which put out *Batman* and *Superman*, and Marvel Comics (an offshoot of Walt Disney since 2009), which first made its name with picture versions of *Spider-Man* and *Captain America*. Both companies (and others) battled in true comic-book hero fashion for supremacy in their field, establishing often confusing 'universes' or even 'multiverses' where characters from different media co-exist on different timelines.

As graphics became easier to reproduce, the names of Sherlock Holmes and related characters proliferated across the comics world. A short-lived magazine titled *Sherlock Holmes* appeared from Charlton Comics in 1955–56. Charlton was snapped up by DC Comics which produced its own magazine called *Sherlock Holmes* in 1975, though strangely its first issue was based on the story 'The Final Problem' which deals with the detective's death. DC Comics also featured Holmes as an adversary of The Joker in strips of that name. Meanwhile canonical figures also appeared in other comic books, such as *The League of Extraordinary Gentlemen*, where the writer Alan Moore and artist Kevin O'Neill introduced Holmes, his brother Mycroft and Professor James Moriarty into storylines from 1999.

Another manifestation was the Japanese manga (in comic strip and comic book form) which built on that country's genius for illustration. One of the best known was *Detective Conan*, which appeared in the *Weekly Shonen Sunday* from 1994 and was collected in over a hundred Tankōbon volumes. Featuring a high-school detective called Shinichi (or Jimmy) Kudo, this series also inspired a long-running anime which has been broadcast over 1,000 times on

Japanese television. For copyright reasons it was known as *Case Closed* in the United States.

Inevitably Conan Doyle's detective was soon featuring in video games. One of the first, which relied on text commands, was *Sherlock*, created by Philip Mitchell of Beam Software and published by Melbourne House, which ran on ZX Spectrum 48K in 1984 and Commodore 64 in 1985. At least nine editions of the video game *Sherlock Holmes*, based on the characters in the Jeremy Brett television series, have been made by Frogworks since 2002 and carry a trademark.

Trademarks suggest the estate was involved in licensing, though it is difficult to follow the exact process. Certainly, many different products are now officially licenced, from greetings cards, through collectibles such as jigsaws, toys and chess figures, to pens in the Writers Collection from Montblanc, where the top-of-the-range white-gold fountain pen retails at £32,000. A glance at the website of the Conan Doyle estate in mid-2022 showed three new entertainment businesses within a couple of months being granted licences to operate using the name Sherlock Holmes. The Original Sherlock Holmes and His Baker Street Irregulars is a crowd-funded board game

Below *This Japanese Foreign Ministry brochure features the cartoon character by the name of 'Detective Conan'.*

for up to five people (manufactured by a company called Baskerville Productions based in Southern Illinois). There's an educational Sherlock Holmes experience at Knockhatch Adventure Park in East Sussex, not far from East Dean, where some commentators have argued the detective retired to in *His Last Bow*. And Universal Studios Japan announced an immersive show called 'Sherlock Holmes: The Curse of the Red Sword', which promised somewhat bizarrely to take visitors 'back to a 1930's Hollywood première and the site of a gruesome and mysterious murder'.

The estate isn't named after Sherlock Holmes, but his creator: Sir Arthur Conan Doyle, so it is worth noting how Holmes's afterlife has been closely linked to Sir Arthur's. It's not that you can't have one without the other, but they feed off each other, so it remains important to have an understanding of his life and work and keep it up to date. Decent biographies can play a role here. Conan Doyle's first official biographer was a Scottish minister called John Lamond who the writer's widow, Lady Jean Conan Doyle, thought could be entrusted with telling the story of an aspect of her husband's life which she held dear – his spiritualist activities. The ensuing volume, published in 1931, was a painful piece of (almost literally) hagiography.

After Lady Jean's death in June 1940, Sir Arthur's heirs, his sons Denis and Adrian, allowed the prolific author Hesketh Pearson to attempt a biography. But they were not happy with the resulting (1943) book which they called a 'fakeography'. They decided they wanted Emil Ludwig, the German-Swiss biographer of Napoleon and Goethe to write their father's life. When he declined Adrian tried his own appreciation, *The True Conan Doyle*, published in 1945. But even he realized there was still something lacking, so the brothers alighted on John Dickson Carr, an author of detective stories, who, like William Gillette, was the son of a US Congressman. Dickson Carr had struck up a friendship with Adrian while negotiating to compile an anthology of Conan Doyle's works. His lively, well-informed but ultimately lightweight biography appeared in 1949, followed five years later by *The Exploits of Sherlock Holmes*, a collection of twelve new stories written in tandem by Adrian and Dickson Carr (six written together, and six by Adrian alone after his partner fell ill). In promoting the book, Adrian stressed how he was drawing on his father's notes and on his personal recollections of his father's comments on his stories. All were based on references to unsolved cases in the canon (a common form of fan fiction). Thus, a story called 'The Adventure of the Two Women' drew on a

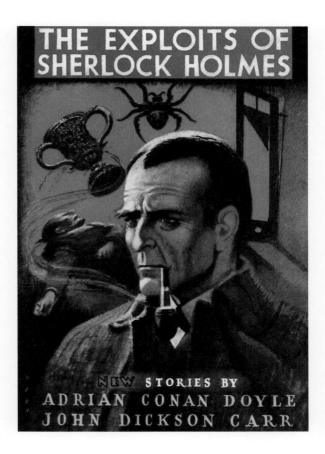

Above The cover of The Exploits of Sherlock Holmes, *a collection of twelve Sherlock Holmes pastiches by Adrian Conan Doyle and John Dickson Carr, published in 1954.*

reference in *The Hound of the Baskervilles* to a case involving a blackmailer which had prevented him from travelling with Watson to Dartmoor – 'At the present instant one of the most revered names in England is being besmirched by a blackmailer, and only I can stop a disastrous scandal.'

Again, Adrian was not satisfied. Having become the manager of the estate following Denis's death in 1955, he wanted a new interpretation of his father's life. In 1959 he once more tried to fill the gap himself with a volume published by John Murray to mark Sir Arthur's centenary. He was helped by a young Frenchman, Pierre Nordon, who was working on a PhD thesis on Conan Doyle. Impressed by Nordon's approach he commissioned him to write a comprehensive biography which appeared in France in 1964 and in the United Kingdom two years later in a translation by Frances Partridge.

Since then, new biographies have followed at regular intervals. They have been aided by the excellent quality of related scholarship. Leading the way were Richard Lancelyn Green and John Michael Gibson who compiled the definitive *A Bibliography of A. Conan Doyle*, originally published in 1983 and revised and expanded in 1999. As well as working on their own individual projects, these two also collaborated on *The Unknown Conan Doyle: Essays on Photography* (1982) which pulled together the author's early articles on his hobby of photography. Another useful contribution from the same era was *The Quest for Sherlock Holmes* by Owen Dudley Edwards (1983).

Serious critical works also helped keep Holmes and his creator new and interesting. One contender in this field was *Sherlock Holmes was Wrong* by the French philosopher Pierre Bayard. Published in 2008, this re-examined the evidence in *The Hound of the Baskervilles* and concluded that the detective had misinterpreted it. The hound was not in any way responsible for the disappearances on the moor which were not the work of his owner Jack Stapleton, the entomologist and would-be heir to the Baskerville inheritance, but of Stapleton's beautiful Costa Rican wife Beryl.

Other important additions to the understanding of Conan Doyle have been editions of unpublished works (such as *The Narrative of John Smith* from the British Library in

Below Martin Clunes as Conan Doyle in the ITV drama Arthur & George, *based on the 2005 novel by Julian Barnes.*

Opposite The House of Silk *(2001) by Anthony Horowitz and* The Beekeeper's Apprentice *(1994) by Laurie R. King.*

2011), a volume of correspondence (*Arthur Conan Doyle: A Life in Letters*, edited by Jon Lellenberg, Daniel Stashower and Charles Foley, 2007), and *A Chronology of the Life of Sir Arthur Conan Doyle* by Brian Pugh (various editions, 2009–18). Further insights have come from new associated biographical material, such as *Out of the Shadows* (2004) by Georgina Doyle who brought family insights as the widow of John Doyle, Sir Arthur's nephew (the son of his brother Innes).

Such works have helped create Conan Doyle as a character in his own right. In the last couple of decades several works of fiction have appeared with him as a central character, including *Arthur & George* by Julian Barnes, published in 2005, which made the shortlist for the Booker Prize. This focused on Conan Doyle's relationship with the wronged Parsee lawyer George Edalji. It spawned a theatre play by David Edgar (2010) and a three-part television series shown on ITV (2015).

Meanwhile, not to be outdone by flashy pastiche, parodies and fanfic, mainstream publishers have returned to the floor with new interpretations of the Holmes stories in volume form. Anthony Horowitz won the backing of the Conan Doyle Estate for his two Sherlock Holmes

continuation novels *The House of Silk* (2011) and *Moriarty* (2014). Anthony Lane wrote several officially endorsed Young Sherlock novels aimed at the young-adult market. And, although not formally sanctioned, a number of feminist-inspired fictional readings have helped realign the generally masculine canon to feminine sensibilities. Holmes has had a female protagonist (a colleague he later marries) in the Mary Russell books written by Laurie R. King, starting with *The Beekeeper's Apprentice* in 1994. Carole Nelson Douglas also extended the Holmesian canon with *Good Night, Mr Holmes*, one of her eight Irene Adler novels, first published in 1990. Holmes has travelled a long way in many people's imaginations since he was first encountered in that chemical laboratory in Bart's Hospital.

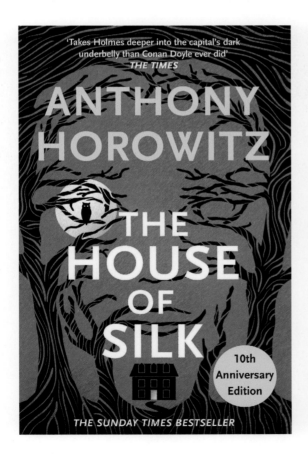

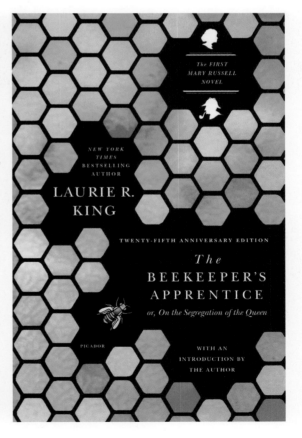

POSTSCRIPT

Holmes had a tricky birth, with Conan Doyle having to hawk the manuscript of *A Study of Scarlet* around several publishers before it found a far-from-lucrative home at *Beeton's Christmas Annual*. But over 130 years later Sherlock Holmes has endured remarkably well.

It's hard to say definitively if he is the world's best-known or even best-loved fictional character. There is no index to provide a reliable answer, but the crowds of tourists who regularly congregate on London's Baker Street suggest he is at least in the top dozen, along with James Bond, Tarzan, Dracula, Winnie-the-Pooh and Alice (in Wonderland). From the world of comics and films, you could add Superman and Mickey Mouse; foreign-language characters would give you the Count of Monte Cristo and Tintin, and offering a historical perspective is Robinson Crusoe. And that's before mentioning the remarkable Harry Potter. But give that lad another century or so and we'll see how he fares.

Sherlock Holmes is a bit different because he works on so many different levels. He's history, narrative, psychology and thriller. And he's wonderfully reassuring, for a start. He solves cases in a methodical but pleasingly ingenious manner. The forces of good (and reason) triumph. His readers (particularly his original commuter ones) can return home and rest safe in their beds at night, knowing that evil and irrationality have been put in their place. That was an important part of his appeal in the 1890s, when Britain's dominant place in the world appeared under threat from countries like Germany, crime loomed darkly in the time of Jack the Ripper, and unruly elements from the subconscious seemed to ready to break loose through the studies of Sigmund Freud.

Yet although Holmes is so much a creature of the fog-ridden age in which he was created, he is also of all times. Part of his appeal is that he is so adaptable, so difficult to pin down. He's a super-sleuth, a 'calculating machine', open to all the signs and clues with which he is presented. He can seem forbiddingly cold, but, despite protestations to the contrary, he is *au fond* an amiable human being who lives cosily with his colleague Dr Watson. This relationship contributes to the detective's continuing attraction. The two men are like a long-suffering married couple, yet one cannot do without the other. And they established the pattern which has endured in detective stories and other narrative forms of the professional team whose members play against and bring out the best of each other.

In his professional life Holmes is sharp but never unkind. Indeed, he is often prepared to take liberties with the law and show lenience to suspected criminals. His empathy comes from being a troubled soul – a depressive who needs at times to turn away from society and lose himself in solitary pursuits, even to the extent of shooting up with cocaine. His mood swings make him a notably modern character, showing evidence of what might today be described as a bipolar personality.

His often-contradictory traits have allowed him to be reinterpreted over the years. They have helped him gain new adherents in different media across the globe (see the chapters in this book about his appearances in film and stage, and also about his strong and steady afterlife where he has found admirers in the worlds of fan fiction and Japanese manga). The words of Vincent Starrett's poem '221B' remain prescient: 'Here dwell together still two men of note/Who never lived and so can never die.'

Opposite The deerstalker and magnifying glass have become iconic of the great detective.

CHRONOLOGY OF CONAN DOYLE AND WORLD EVENTS

1854 Start of the Crimean War. Birth of Oscar Wilde.

1859 22 May, birth of Arthur Conan Doyle in Edinburgh.

1859 Publication of Charles Darwin's *On the Origin of Species*.

1861 Start of the American Civil War.

1863 Metropolitan Railway opens in London.

1866 ACD attends Newington Academy, Edinburgh.

1867 Second Reform Bill (franchises extended) in Britain.

1868 ACD attends Hodder preparatory school, Lancashire.

1870 ACD enters Stonyhurst College, Lancashire. 9 June, death of Charles Dickens.

1875 ACD spends year at Jesuit school in Feldkirch, Austria.

1876 ACD enters Edinburgh University to study medicine.

1879 September, ACD's first story 'The Mystery of the Sasassa Valley' published in *Chambers Journal*, and his first non-fiction 'Gelseminum as a Poison' in the *British Medical Journal*.

1880 ACD serves as ship's doctor on whaling ship *Hope* in the Arctic.

1881 ACD graduates MB. The Doyle family is now living at 15 Lonsdale Terrace Edinburgh. Sails (October) to West Africa as ship's doctor on SS *Mayumba*.

1882 After false start with his old friend George Budd in Plymouth, ACD enters general practice in Southsea. Publishes in *London Society*, *All the Year Round*, *The Lancet*, and the *British Journal of Photography*.

1882 ACD's father Charles Altamont Doyle institutionalized as a result of his alcoholism. His mother Mary moves to Masongill Cottage on Yorkshire estate of Dr Bryan Waller who had lodged with the family while he was studying medicine in Edinburgh. From September ACD's brother Innes helps out in his surgery as a page.

1883 January, 'The Captain of the Pole-Star' published in *Temple Bar*.

1884 Further publications including 'J. Habakuk Jephson's Statement' (*Cornhill Magazine*).

1885 26 January, death of General Gordon in Khartoum. 23 June, Conservative party under Lord Salisbury takes power in Britain. August, ACD marries Louise ('Touie') Hawkins. Travels to Ireland on honeymoon (playing cricket).

1887 *A Study in Scarlet* published in *Beeton's Christmas Annual*. Queen Victoria's Golden Jubilee.

1888 Jack the Ripper killings in Whitechapel, London. December, *A Study in Scarlet* published in book form by Ward, Lock. *The Mystery of Cloomber* published.

1889 February, *Micah Clarke*, ACD's novel about the Monmouth Rebellion, published. Dinner in Langham's Hotel leads to commissioning of *The Sign of (the) Four* by *Lippincott's*. Daughter Mary Louise born.

1890 March, *The Sign of the Four* published in *Lippincott's*. October, *The Firm of Girdlestone* published.

1891 ACD moves to London to establish himself as an eye specialist. Initially lives in Montague Place, with rooms at 2 Upper Wimpole Street. Published *A Scandal in Bohemia* is published. ACD quits medicine to write full time. Moves to South Norwood.

1892 15 August, Gladstone becomes Prime Minister for the fourth time. 6 October, death of Alfred, Lord Tennyson. 31 October, *The Adventures of Sherlock Holmes*, ACD's first collection of his stories published in book form by Newnes. Son Arthur Alleyne Kingsley born.

1893 10 October, death of Charles Altamont Doyle. December, second collection of stories, *The Memoirs of Sherlock Holmes* published.

1894 5 March, Lord Rosebery becomes Prime Minister. *Round the Red Lamp* (a collection of medical stories) is published in October, followed by *The Parasite* in December. ACD visits the United States on a lecture tour with his brother Innes. The first Brigadier Gerard story, 'The Medal of Brigadier Gerard' published in *The Strand Magazine*. Dreyfus case begins in France.

1895 ACD and Louise visit Egypt. *The Stark Munro Letters* published. Lord Salisbury again Prime Minister. Lumière Brothers hold first public film exhibitions in Paris. Sino-Japanese War.

1896 February, *The Exploits of Brigadier Gerard* published. April, first modern Olympics held in Athens. November, *Rodney Stone* published.

1897 ACD moves with his family to Hindhead in Surrey. Falls in love with Jean Leckie. Napoleonic novel *Uncle Bernac* published. Queen Victoria's Diamond Jubilee.

1898 February, *The Tragedy of the Korosko* published. Spanish-American War. Fashoda Crisis. June, book of verses, *Songs of Action*, published. 2 September, Kitchener defeats Mahdists at Battle of Omdurman.

1899 William Gillette starts to portray Sherlock Holmes on the stage. ACD joins Langman's Hospital in South African (Boer) War.

1900 ACD writes *The Great Boer War*, stands as unsuccessful Liberal Unionist candidate for Edinburgh Central. August, *The Hound of the Baskervilles* begins serialization in *Strand*.

1901 Death of Queen Victoria, succeeded by King Edward VII.

1902 January, *The War in South Africa, Its Cause and Its Conduct* published. ACD knighted. *The Hound of the Baskervilles* published in book form by Newnes. 11 July, Lord Salisbury steps down as Prime Minister and leader of the Conservative party and is succeeded by Arthur Balfour

1903 September, *Adventures of Gerard* published by Newnes. October, Sherlock Holmes re-emerges in 'The Empty House', in the *Strand*.

1904 Anglo-French Entente Cordiale.

1905 March *The Return of Sherlock Holmes* published by Newnes. 5 December, the Liberal party leader Sir Henry Campbell-Bannerman succeeds Arthur Balfour as Prime Minister.

1906 Death of Louise Doyle. ACD takes up the Edalji case. ACD defeated as Liberal Unionist candidate in Hawick District.

1907 Robert Baden-Powell founds the Boy Scouts. November, ACD marries Jean Leckie. Publishes *Through the Magic Door*, about his favourite books.

1908 5 April, Herbert Asquith succeeds Sir Henry Campbell-Bannerman as Prime Minister and leader of the Liberal Party. ACD moves to Windlesham, Crowborough, Sussex.

1909 ACD becomes President of the Divorce Law Reform Union. Birth of son Denis. Begins to campaign on the Congo.

1910 ACD takes a six-month lease on the Adelphi Theatre in London. His play *The Speckled Band* runs there for 346 performances. Son Adrian born.

1912 'The Lost World', the first Professor Challenger story, published in *Strand*. Birth of daughter Jean. The sinking of the *Titanic*. Ronald Knox publishes *Studies in the Literature of Sherlock Holmes*.

1913 ACD writes *Great Britain and the Next War* published February in *Fortnightly Review*. Campaigns for a channel tunnel.

1914 ACD and Jean tour the United States and Canada. At the start of war against Germany, ACD organizes local volunteer force.

1915 February, *The Valley of Fear* published in US (June in UK). ACD embarks on history of the British campaign in France and Flanders (published 1916).

1916 Battle of Jutland. 6 December, David Lloyd George succeeds Herbert Asquith as Prime Minister and Leader of the Liberal Party.

1917 Appeals for clemency for his friend Sir Roger Casement, who has been convicted of High Treason. *His Last Bow* published in *Strand*, and later in book form by John Murray

1918 April, *The New Revelation* published. ACD is now a fully-fledged spiritualist. 28 October, death of his son Kingsley. Armistice. Kaiser Wilhelm abdicates.

1919 Death of brother Innes from Spanish 'flu. Versailles peace treaty. Weimar Republic established in Germany.

1920 Friendship with Houdini. Photographs of the Cottingley Fairies published. Australian lecture tour.

1921 Death of ACD's mother Mary. Stoll Pictures begins its series of Sherlock Holmes films.

1922 ACD's Spiritualist tour of North America. 20 May, Prime Minister David Lloyd George resigns, to be succeeded by Andrew Bonar Law. Benito Mussolini becomes Prime Minister of Italy.

1923 22 May, Stanley Baldwin succeeds Bonar Law as Prime Minister.

1924 *Memories and Adventures* published. Ramsay MacDonald forms the first Labour administration, but Baldwin soon succeeds him after a general election. The Zinoviev letter is published.

1925 ACD publishes *History of Spiritualism* and *The Land of Mist*, a spiritualist novel featuring Professor Challenger. Adolf Hitler publishes the first volume of *Mein Kampf*.

1926 Birth of Princess Elizabeth, later Queen Elizabeth II.

1927 June, *The Casebook of Sherlock Holmes* published by John Murray.

1928 ACD travels with his family to Africa.

1929 ACD visits Holland and Scandinavia. *The Maracot Deep* and *Our African Winter* published.

1930 July 7, death of ACD.

1934 Baker Street Irregulars first meet. Sherlock Holmes Society of London formed.

1939 Basil Rathbone plays Sherlock Holmes in *The Hound of the Baskervilles*.

1940 27 June, death of Jean Conan Doyle.

***c*.1967** Adventuresses of Sherlock Holmes formed.

1970 Billy Wilder directs *The Private Life of Sherlock Holmes*.

1984 Granada Television's series *The Adventures of Sherlock Holmes* airs, starring Jeremy Brett. It runs over forty-five episodes until 1994.

1985 Barry Levinson directs *Young Sherlock Holmes*.

2009 Warner Brothers releases feature film *Sherlock Holmes* starring Robert Downey Jr. and Jude Law.

2010 The BBC series *Sherlock* first appears, starring Benedict Cumberbatch.

2011 Anthony Horowitz's continuation novel *The House of Silk* published.

CHRONOLOGY OF HOLMES AND WATSON

The dating of the Sherlock Homes stories is highly contentious. Certain events can be placed with precision – either an actual date is mentioned in the text, or it relates to something else in the canon. Other occurrences are more hazy, and still more have to be left to guesswork.

The following draws on dates provided in a number of sources – notably the *New Annotated Sherlock Holmes* edited by Leslie S. Klinger; *My Dear Holmes* by Gavin Brend; *The Chronological Holmes* by William S. Baring-Gould, and *Quel jour sommes-nous, Watson* by Jean-Pierre Crauser.

1846	Birth of James Moriarty.
1847	Birth of Mycroft Holmes.
***c.*1852**	Birth of John Watson.
1854	Birth of Sherlock Holmes.
1872	Watson begins his medical studies at St Bartholomew's Hospital, London.
***c.*1872**	Holmes goes to University, (possibly Christ Church, Oxford), from where, after two years, he leaves without a degree.
1873	The *Gloria Scott* sails and is destroyed.
***c.*1874**	Watson is appointed a houseman at St Bartholomew's Hospital, London, where Stamford acts as his dresser.
***c.*1875**	Holmes in lodgings in Montague Street, studying further in the British Museum Library and at St Bartholomew's.
1878	Holmes investigates the strange disappearance of Musgrave's missing servants and discovers the lost crown of King Charles I. Watson takes his degree of Doctor of Medicine at the University of London, goes to Netley to train as an army surgeon.
1879	Watson joins the 5th Northumberland Fusiliers in Afghanistan.
1880	Watson wounded at the Battle of Maiwand.
1881	1 January, Watson meets Stamford at the Criterion Bar in Piccadilly and is introduced to Sherlock Holmes. The two men cohabit in 221B Baker Street. Holmes publishes *The Book of Life*. March, *A Study in Scarlet*.
1882	March, 'The Yellow Face'. Summer, 'The Greek Interpreter'. December, 'Charles Augustus Milverton'.
1883	April, 'The Speckled Band'.
1886	March, 'The Beryl Coronet'. Autumn, 'The Second Stain'. Holmes publishes *On Variations in the Human Ear*.

1887 Holmes suffering 'from the strain caused by his immense exertions' that spring. April, 'The Reigate Squires'. July, *The Sign of Four*. August, 'The Cardboard Box'. September/October, 'Silver Blaze'. October 'The Noble Bachelor' and 'The Resident Patient'.

1888 Watson marries Mary Morstan. 20 March, Watson returns from his practice to visit Holmes at the start of 'A Scandal in Bohemia'. June, 'The Stockbroker's Clerk'. July, 'The Naval Treaty'. August, 'The Crooked Man'. September, 'The Five Orange Pips'.

1889 Watson practising in Paddington. 'The Engineer's Thumb'. March, 'Scandal in Bohemia'. April, 'A Case of Identity'. June, 'The Man with the Twisted Lip' and 'The Boscombe Valley Mystery'. November, 'The Dying Detective'. December, 'The Blue Carbuncle'.

1890 Watson moves to a new practice in Kensington. March, 'The Copper Beeches'. October, 'The Red-Headed League'.

1891 April, 'The Final Problem'. Death of Moriarty at the Reichenbach Falls. Holmes, apparently dead, travels widely in Asia, Africa and Europe during his three year long 'great hiatus'.

***c.*1893** Death of Mrs Watson.

1894 February, 'The Empty House'. March, 'Wisteria Lodge'. August, 'The Norwood Builder'. November, 'The Golden Pince-Nez'.

1895 Dr Verner buys Watson's practice and Watson returns to Baker Street. April, 'The Solitary Cyclist'. May, 'The Three Students'. July, 'Black Peter'. November, 'The Bruce-Partington Plans'. Holmes travels to Windsor to receive the gift of an emerald tie pin from Queen Victoria for his role in recovering the Bruce-Partington submarine plans. Holmes working on his monograph *On Polyphonic Motets of Lassus*.

1896 January, 'The Red Circle'. October, 'The Veiled Lodger'. November, 'The Sussex Vampire'.

1897 Holmes retires to Cornwall to recuperate. January, 'The Abbey Grange'. March, 'The Devil's Foot'. December, 'The Missing Three-Quarter'.

1898 'The Dancing Man' and 'The Retired Colourman'.

1899 'The Disappearance of Lady Frances Carfax'. October, *The Hound of the Baskervilles*.

1900 'The Six Napoleons'. January, *The Valley of Fear*. October, 'Thor Bridge'.

1901 May, 'The Priory School'.

1902 May, 'Shoscombe Old Place'. June, 'The Three Garridebs'. September, 'The Illustrious Client'.

1903 'The Mazarin Stone'. January, 'The Blanched Soldier'. June, 'The Three Gables'. September, 'The Creeping Man'. Holmes retires to Sussex where he keeps bees. Watson said to be remarried and working in Queen Anne Street.

1907 'The Lion's Mane'.

1912 Holmes pursues a German spy ring, a mission which takes him to the United States. August, Holmes summons Watson to help with capture of Von Bork.

1914 August, *His Last Bow*.

FURTHER READING

Allan, Janice M. and Pittard, Christopher (eds), *The Cambridge Companion to Sherlock Holmes* (Cambridge, 2019).

Bayard, Pierre, *Sherlock Holmes was Wrong* (Bloomsbury, 2010).

Black, Jeremy, *The Game is Afoot* (Rowman & Littlefield, 2022).

Bostrom, Mattias, *The Life and Death of Sherlock Holmes* (Head of Zeus, 2017).

Clausson, Nils (ed.), *Re-examining Arthur Conan Doyle* (Cambridge Scholars Publishing, 2021).

Conan Doyle, Arthur, *Memories and Adventures* (Hodder & Stoughton, 1924).

Conan Doyle, Arthur, *The Narrative of John Smith* (British Library, 2011).

Conan Doyle, Arthur, *Through the Magic Door* (Smith, Elder & Co., 1907).

Conan Doyle, Arthur (general editor Owen Dudley Edwards), *The Oxford Sherlock Holmes* (Oxford, 1993).

Cox, Michael (ed.), *The Baker Street File* (Calabash Press, 2002).

Frank, Lawrence, *Victorian Detective Fiction and the Nature of Evidence: The Scientific Investigations of Poe, Dickens and Doyle* (Palgrave Macmillan, 2003).

Hall, Trevor H., *Sherlock Holmes and His Creator* (Gerald Duckworth, 1978).

Holmes, John and Ruston, Sharon (eds), *The Routledge Research Companion to Nineteenth Century British Literature and Science* (Routledge, 2017).

Keating, H.R.F., *Sherlock Holmes: The Man and His World* (Thames & Hudson, 1979).

Kerr, Douglas, *Conan Doyle: Writing, Profession and Practice* (Oxford University Press, 2013).

Klinger, Leslie S. (ed.), *The New Annotated Sherlock Holmes* (W.W. Norton, 2006).

Knight, Stephen, *Crime Fiction 1800–2000* (Palgrave, 2004).

Lancelyn Green, Richard and Gibson, John Michael, *A Bibliography of A. Conan Doyle* (Hudson House, 2000).

Lellenberg, Jon, Stashower, Dan and Foley, Charles, *Arthur Conan Doyle: A Life in Letters* (HarperPress, 2008).

Lycett, Andrew, *Conan Doyle: The Man Who Created Sherlock Holmes* (Weidenfeld & Nicolson, 2007)

Lycett, Andrew (ed.), *Conan Doyle's Wide World* (Tauris Peake, 2020).

Miller, D.A., *The Novel and the Police* (University of California Press, 1988).

Miranker, Cathy and Glen, *Sherlock Holmes in 221 Objects* (The Grolier Club, 2022).

O'Brien, James, *The Scientific Sherlock Holmes* (Oxford University Press, 2013).

Pugh, Brian W., *A Chronology of the Life of Sir Arthur Conan Doyle* (MX Publishing, 2018).

Richards, Dana (ed.), *My Scientific Methods: Science in the Sherlockian Canon* (Baker Street Irregulars, 2022).

Rzepka, Charles J., *Detective Fiction* (Polity Press, 2005).

Steinbrunner, Chris and Michaels, Norman, *The Films of Sherlock Holmes* (Citadel Press, 1978).

Stuart Davies, David, *Holmes at the Movies* (New English Library, 1976).

Tracy, Jack, *The Ultimate Sherlock Holmes Encyclopedia* (Gramercy Books, 1977).

Utechin, Nicholas, *Amazing & Extraordinary Facts: Sherlock Holmes* (David & Charles, 2012).

Vanacker, Sabine and Wynne, Catherine (eds), *Sherlock Holmes and Conan Doyle: Multi-Media Afterlives* (Palgrave Macmillan, 2013).

Wagner, E.J., *The Science of Sherlock Holmes* (John Wiley & Sons, 2006).

Werner, Alex (ed.), *Sherlock Holmes: The Man Who Never Lived and Will Never Die* (Ebury Press, 2014).

White, Jerry, *London in the Nineteenth Century* (Jonathan Cape, 2007).

Wynne, Catherine, *The Colonial Conan Doyle: British Imperialism, Irish Nationalism and the Gothic* (Greenwood Press, 2002).

Other sources

Scuttlebutt from the Spermaceti Press.

The Arthur Conan Doyle Encyclopaedia: https://www.arthur-conan-doyle.com/index.php/Main_Page

The Baker Street Journal (publication of the Baker Street Irregulars).

The Sherlock Holmes Journal (publication of the Sherlock Holmes Society of London).

INDEX

PICTURE CREDITS

Quarto

Publisher Philip Cooper
Commissioning Editor John Parton
Senior Editor Michael Brunström
Art Director Paileen Currie
Designer Glenn Howard
Production Controller Rohana Yusof

Acknowledgments

I am hugely grateful to Catherine Cooke and Peter Horrocks
from the Sherlock Holmes Society of London. They have
combed through my text and pointed out the most egregious
mistakes in what I originally wrote. Many thanks also to David
Richards, who read my draft from a slightly different (historian's)
perspective. I am, of course, responsible for any errors which
remain. Others who have helped me in different ways on both
sides of the Atlantic Ocean include Steven Rothman, Calvert
Markham, Matt Wingett, Cliff Goldfarb, Roger Johnson and
Mark Jones. And I must acknowledge the general (and genial)
encouragement over the years of that pre-eminent Sherlockian,
the now sadly much-missed Nick Utechin.